LAUGHING HYENAS

BOOKS BY STEVE MILLER

A Slaying in the Suburbs: The Tara Grant Murder

Girl, Wanted: The Chase for Sarah Pender

*Nobody's Women: The Crimes and Victims of Anthony Sowell,
the Cleveland Serial Killer*

*Murder in Grosse Pointe Park: Privilege, Adultery,
and the Killing of Jane Bashara*

*Touch and Go: The Complete Hardcore
Punk Zine '79-'83 (editor)*

*Detroit Rock City: The Uncensored History of Rock 'n' Roll
in America's Loudest City*

Juggalo: Insane Clown Posse and the World They Made

LAUGHING HYENAS

Steve Miller

J-Card
Press

ISBN 979-8-9917394-0-5 (print)
ISBN 979-8-9917394-1-2 (ebook)

Library of Congress Control Number: 2025933576

J-Card Press
460 Center Street #6578
Moraga, California 94570

Cover photo by Rick McGinnis
Designed by Ana Cenador
Author photo by Nicole Rico

www.jcardpress.com

CONTENTS

INTRO

The Laughing Hyenas were the last of the original rock 'n' roll bands.

They heeded no caution. Reality first, safety last, laying down music that was uncompromising, brutal, and heartfelt.

Where do you find that today?

Rock 'n' roll was a movement started by rebels, outlaws, and misfits creating music that didn't play by the rules. These progenitors behaved with a reckless abandon that mortified the straights and earned the admiration of fellow travelers.

The Hyenas did drugs, went to jail, and lived the lives of gypsies while touring hand to mouth, thankful for their five-dollars-a-day stipend, traveling the country in a dilapidated van.

They drove through snowstorms, droughts, and downpours, often with spotty heat or air-conditioning in their vehicle, just to spend forty minutes a night delivering the goods. It didn't matter if that set was played for five or five hundred people, the Hyenas played for their lives, purging the sounds that rang in their heads every day. A Hyenas show between 1989 and 1991 was an aural wrecking crew.

It's not a stretch to contend that such dedicated adherence

to music is on pause today, as so much music has become an economic equation. And drugs of course still exist, although you're more likely to find the emboldened, sanctioned Big Pharma dispensing it rather than a shady street hustler.

Many artists over the years grabbed onto heroin, which played a role in the Hyenas aura, as both a key to creativity—a valid although socially distasteful fact—and a crutch to deal with the complication of existence. No one asked to be here. It can be frustrating and puzzling, depending on your level of consciousness.

The Laughing Hyenas could not exist today. Too much danger, too many risks, and not enough cash return.

For cofounder John Brannon, it took courage to change musical direction abruptly, as he did, from the narrowness of hardcore to the blues and jazz-based damage of the Hyenas.

Punk rock was a reaction to the sameness of traditional music. It was a black iron fist to the midsection of the beige corporate sounds that were chart-toppers in the late seventies. But it did its job, changing the direction of both music and culture, before sinking into the same big-business nothingness it sought to destroy.

Green Day et al. were admirably doing their thing for a minute before the suits swooped in. Today, punk rock is Ticketmaster stadium fodder.

It took a while for it to fade. But Brannon was ahead of the curve.

"When the Hyenas started, it was probably about 1985, Negative Approach was over, hardcore was probably in my mind over, and I discovered the blues and the Birthday Party and was just into different music," Brannon told music journalist Tony Rettman in an unpublished 2010 interview. "An early Black Flag gig, it might've been their last tour, they played at Traxx. It might've been our second gig with the Hyenas, and we were still learning how to play. Larissa had probably been playing guitar for six months. L-Seven broke up, so I was like, 'Both our bands broke up, why don't we start a band, you play guitar.' And the kids would be like, 'Can't Tell No One,' and they really couldn't accept that I was trying to do something different, because it was still a young crowd going out to see Black Flag. And I was coming up with something completely different that wasn't hardcore. I had long hair, doing a freaked-out blues noise punk thing, or whatever they called it. I got a lot of shit for that, but I was more happy doing this and moving on than trying to hold on to something that's so over. And to this day, a lot of those records I still feel really good about."

That's a musical integrity that's hard to fathom, especially as it came at a time when the goal of many bands was to land a contract with the big-label masters, get enough money to not have to work, and sail into some sort of fame game.

SIDE 1

"Hey, come on now, let's get that muggles going."

John Brannon took a long pull on a short joint, paused, then exhaled.

Inside his head, there was nothing beyond his closed eyes. Just the smoke, the sizzling feedback from the guitar amp behind him, and darkness.

The Laughing Hyenas were holding court in a cramped basement in East Lansing, Michigan, an exuberant Midwestern college town. The elbow-to-elbow crowd of fifty people furiously puffed on cigarettes and pounded cheap beer from red Solo party cups, some of the taller attendees scraping their heads on the low ceiling. What was a code inspector's nightmare was a dream come true for Brannon and the Hyenas, who ignited crowds with an intoxicated, brooding fusion of rock, blues, and free jazz.

It was October 1989, and the Hyenas were playing songs from a growing catalog, having released their first album, *You Can't Pray a Lie*, in March. The noise was cacophony, a bass-led blare. Brannon sang through a couple of monitor wedges turned toward the room. The band stood almost as tightly as the crowd, and occasionally a drunken member of the audience stepped on the Tube Driver pedal used by guitarist Larissa Strickland, stopping her crusade in mid-chord.

It was just part of the game for the Hyenas, who were bent on playing every basement, squat, and dumpster club that would have them.

"We didn't want to be a hometown band," says Kevin Monroe, the band's bassist. "But we would take party gigs in smaller towns around the area where people might not always get a chance to see us."

On this night, like so many others, the band raged, then packed up its gear, pocketed some cash, and got in the van.

The forty-five-minute drive back to their rented brick house, set on a quarter-acre corner lot in Ann Arbor, was punctuated by the glow of lit cigarettes and the pop of opening beer cans.

It was pretty good work for the $200 in damp dollar bills they were paid.

They couldn't wait to do it again, which they would, over and over, until they developed a devoted following of true believers.

The Hyenas were preaching the gospel, a new twist on the punk rock that Brannon had once called the "soul music of the suburbs."

The band was a quartet of individuals linked by a mission to wreak musical havoc. Brannon was the son of a preacher, like his musical hero Alice Cooper. The family—Brannon, his older sister, and his mother—moved from Pontiac, Michigan, where Brannon was born, to New Jersey and back to Michigan as his dad took pastoral jobs where he could find them, until finally settling in Grosse Pointe Park, spitting distance from Detroit. His parents divorced when Brannon was nine years old, and his mom raised her two children on her own, working as a secretary.

John Brannon, 6 or 7 years old, taken at Call of The Wild museum in Gaylord, Michigan. "My Grandma used to take me there."
Courtesy of Julie Jumonville.

They couldn't have landed in a better place. The town was a twenty-minute drive to the heart of downtown, but in terms of demographics it was a different universe. The Grosse Pointe block of five small towns were monied, filled with nuclear families headed by auto executives, state government honchos, and the occasional Mob lieutenant. Some of the older homes had escape tunnels running underneath, where members of the Detroit Partnership and the Purple Gang, two of the city's most violent and ambitious organized crime groups that prospered beginning in the early twentieth century, would escape if needed.

Brannon graduated from Grosse Pointe South High School in 1979, ready to make it big with his first band, Static, an outfit that rolled the fashion of New York Dolls in with the guitar chops of the Sweet. He was the lead vocalist and a born leader, full of charisma and a voice that merged control and rage.

His next ensemble was Negative Approach, formed as hardcore punk rock became a suitable alternative to the watered-down new wave that corporate labels were flocking to in 1981. After an album, an EP, and some tours, Negative Approach called it a day. Brannon was ready for something new.

Larissa Strickland was born Larissa Stolarchuk in New Castle, Pennsylvania, to first-generation Ukrainian immigrants. She was the middle of three children, with an older brother and younger sister. The family, led by her father Nestor, a bishop in the Ukrainian Orthodox Church, moved to Detroit when she was young, settling in Southfield, a working-class suburb. Strickland was art-minded from the start and blossomed as a student, taking classes at the Parsons School of Design in New York City.

Pursuing her love of heavy-duty rock 'n' roll, Strickland began attending shows and making friends.

She jumped into the scene as the vocalist of the Detroit band L-Seven, but her reputation was much broader. Strickland was known for being known, for "just being Larissa," Michael Smith, drummer in L-Seven, said.

L-Seven released a single and landed some prime opening

slots, including bills with the Stranglers, Killing Joke, and Bauhaus.

She met Brannon through the emerging hardcore scene. They became close quickly, bonding over a love of intoxication and good music.

Larissa Strickland at the house on Platt Road. Photo by Kevin Monroe.

By 1981, they were a couple, living in a Cass Corridor dump, dubbed the Clubhouse, with no running water. The Cass Corridor neighborhood was a roiling circus of street crime with a history of music relevance. *Creem* magazine was headquartered there in its infancy, and several clubs, from empty storefronts to professional drinking bars, operated in and around the corridor.

When L-Seven ended, she and Brannon roamed, squatting or for meager rent, in several low-life spots in Detroit. By the time they moved to Ann Arbor, through some serious listening and experiencing a pivotal live show, they had the inspiration to create something altogether different.

Kevin Monroe, bassist, was the son of a heralded Detroit Symphony Orchestra flutist, an enthusiastic learner, and, like Strickland, a lover of art. Born in the heart of Detroit, his family moved to Grosse Pointe when he was in the eighth grade. Monroe attended Grosse Pointe South High School as a freshman when Brannon was a senior. When Brannon's band Static played the high school gym, Monroe was there. He liked the spirit but was a Hendrix guy at the time, being a guitar player.

Kevin Monroe at W.J. Maxey Boys Training School, Whitmore Lake, Michigan, 1985. Courtesy of Kevin Monroe.

"I hated high school and thought it was a waste of time," Monroe says. He wanted to learn his own way and lived on the periphery of the emerging hardcore scene that Brannon was quickly ruling, as Negative Approach played on almost every bill featuring a national hardcore act. Monroe's entrée into the scene blossoming around Cass Corridor was through his friendship with Veronica Webb, a local actress and model he met while attending Detroit Waldorf School, a private school, for a couple years before going to high school.

"She knew John and Larissa, and she would go to the shows," Monroe says.

Monroe learned more about Brannon and Strickland, knowing them as a bohemian Bonnie and Clyde.

Monroe met them more formally when they were looking for a bass player for a new project they were putting together. He would be glad to switch from guitar to be a part of it. It was an adventure.

Jim Kimball, the drummer, was best known for his Ann Arbor pedigree and lineage. His older brother, Bruce, was an Olympic diver who won the silver in 1984. Jim's father was a diving legend, coaching the US Olympic diving teams five times between 1964 and 1992, while also serving as the diving coach of the nationally regarded University of Michigan diving team.

Jim, as the youngest of three children, went into diving for a while but was less inclined to follow his elders. Instead, in the fourth grade, he decided to become a drummer and followed his love of music. He played around the area, landing in jazz bands and new wave combos that allowed him to learn precision. He was a natural loner, a lover of nature and dogs, and was curious enough to answer an ad seeking a drummer put up by Brannon and Strickland at the local Schoolkids record store. Kimball was the youngest of the Hyenas, at twenty-three. But he wanted to be part of something bigger than a local act, and once they accepted him, he was ready to roll with whatever path looked good.

After the basement show in East Lansing, they drove home with the cassette deck playing something, anything from Son House, cigarettes glowing in the dark van, Strickland driving. Their ears rang slightly from the relentless volume in a basement space. By the time the band's van pulled into their rented band house at 3416 Platt Road, it was too late to move the gear into the basement, where they practiced. The area was safe, and it could wait until the next afternoon. They unfolded from the van and, like soldiers returning from another mission, headed to their bunks.

Detroit's hardcore scene was one of the best in the US, outstripping that of Chicago, New York, and Washington, DC, and influenced by the trendsetting Los Angeles sound.

The coverage of Detroit was led by a magazine, *Touch and Go*, based in Michigan's dilapidated capital city of Lansing. It was run by two feisty suburbanites, public school teacher Bob Vermeulen, who nicknamed himself Tesco Vee, and former high school football star Dave Stimson. The magazine tracked all things punk rock and more, displaying an insouciance that attracted and repelled but most importantly documented an emerging musical revolution locally and globally.

Vee and Stimson parlayed the magazine into a DIY record label that served up now-collectible seven-inch records by Midwest hardcore bands including the Fix, Necros, and

Vee's band the Meatmen, which was less hard, more core.

By late 1981, the label was being run by Corey Rusk, bass player in the Necros, who quickly began expanding. Among the first new bands courted was Brannon's Negative Approach.

"Corey took over the label and wanted to put out a split single, Negative Approach and the Meatmen, but I didn't want to do that," Brannon says. "I just wanted NA as its own, and Corey was like 'Aaaa.' But I think it worked out better for everyone."

A Negative Approach seven-inch ten-song EP came out in mid-1982 on Touch and Go.

Brannon was already a leader in the scene, followed by others while he himself looked up to bands like the Misfits and Black Flag, whom NA shared the stage with on numerous occasions. Brannon was a walking quote machine, uttering and writing youthful slogans like "long hair is old man's hair," told to indie mag *Trashland Adventures*, a credo he spouted on more than one occasion.

Brannon was often accompanied by Strickland, an "it" girl of Detroit's hardcore scene. He approached her after seeing her at shows.

"We talked about upcoming gigs, her magazine, that kind of shit," he says.

They hit it off and always connected from then on, talking whenever they saw each other at the growing number of shows in the Detroit area.

"She really stood out, really looked unique," Brannon says. Strickland's band L-Seven featured crafty art damage, ahead-of-the-pack musicianship, and bad attitudes. "We went and saw her band play; they got some good gigs, like opening for Bauhaus at [local club] Bookies. This was before Negative Approach. She was ahead of me. She was the coolest chick in Detroit."

Everyone noticed her, with her bleached mop of blond hair, smooth Eastern European white skin, and thrift-store fashions, anchored by a ragged pair of combat boots. She was always carrying things: bags of records, tapes, and an impressive number of fanzines, including *Touch and Go*.

"She had a million fanzines," Smith, the L-Seven drummer, told *Detroit Metro Times* in 2020. "My God, I was hip to fanzines, but she was like an addict." A prescient description; Strickland was already experimenting with heroin, which would burden her the rest of her days.

Strickland was ubiquitous and insistent. There she was at the after-party of a Black Flag show in Lansing in March 1981, chatting up Black Flag bassist Chuck Dukowski, who possessed encyclopedic knowledge of places to play and touring strategy in the nascent stages of the hardcore scene.

"Chuck Dukowski and Black Flag laid down American touring as the world knows it," Brannon says. Strickland knew it as well and used her considerable charm to cultivate friendships as she moved through the music scene.

A year later, she captured the crowd's attention as she repeatedly dove boots-first into the audience at a Flipper show at Ann Arbor's Second Chance.

Everyone saw her at every show; she was impossible to miss.

In an early L-Seven interview with Tesco Vee in *Touch and Go*, she ticked off her musical favorites, a buffet of good taste: "Criminal Class, Alice Cooper, Negative Approach, T. Rex, 4-Skins with [vocalist] Hodges, Motörhead, Iron Fist, Anti-Nowhere League, L-Seven, Upstarts, Deep Purple, Birthday Party, Last Resort, Slade, all Touch and Go efforts, Joy Division, Venom, Static, Meat Puppets, Sweet, more

Alice Cooper, Rainbow, Infa Riot, the Strike, Red Alert, Necros, Blitz, SOA, Redd Kross, Germs, Leather Nun, Killing Joke."

Strickland's mid-1981 connect with Brannon began when she was living in Cass Corridor. Brannon had been unceremoniously booted from his mom's home in Grosse Pointe.

"My mom chased me out of the house with a hammer because I had a Necros/Bored Youth gig in my mom's basement," Brannon says. "The gig had been booked at Nunzios, and I brought thirty to forty little skinhead derelicts home for the show. She was out of town, but she came home, and the next day she said, 'You're moving.'"

He knew where he wanted to be. He hopped on the #9 Jefferson bus, and in an hour he was at Strickland's doorstep.

"What's up?" Brannon said. He'd met her enough times, and he was a known quantity in the scene. "I need a place to stay."

"Come on in," Strickland said.

In short order, they learned about each other, trading secrets and exchanging plans. Each of them had been told to fuck off by almost every landlord, boss, and teacher in their life until the feeling was mutual.

They were together as romantic partners for a decade.

On March 25, 1983, the Birthday Party hit the stage at Traxx, a former biker bar and weathered nightclub on the north side of Detroit. Starting with "Hamlet," off the band's second and final album, *Junkyard*, the show changed the trajectory of Detroit rock music and, more specifically, the musical ideology of Brannon.

The Birthday Party were nearing the end of an influential reign that began in Melbourne, Australia, in 1978, and continued as the band moved to London, where it ended, following the tour that included the Detroit show.

Led by singer Nick Cave, who was hardly the most important member of the band—that would be guitarist Rowland Howard—the Birthday Party made a noisy, bluesy cacophony that was delivered in a confrontational live show.

In Detroit, that show lasted forty-five minutes. It was all Brannon needed.

This is the future of rock 'n' roll, he thought to himself. *This makes sense to me, this is the genius of everything, including hardcore, together.*

Added to the allure, L-Seven opened the show, and Brannon and Strickland got to talk with Cave. While they were listeners and fans before the Traxx show, in the wake of the Birthday Party's raucous set, Cave became godlike to them. Brannon immediately decided he would grow his hair into a dark, greasy mop, which looked strikingly like Cave's coif-ish do.

The next day at Negative Approach practice, Brannon's bandmates, who were at the show, were unimpressed.

"I really hated that band," one of them said.

"No, I'm telling you right now, this is it, the future," Brannon countered. "I have seen it."

Brannon was joined in his admiration by Kevin Monroe, who'd been listening to the Birthday Party for the last year or so. The band looked great, he thought, and that was a good first step. When he heard them, the deal was sealed.

Monroe, too, was thinking of how cool it would be to incorporate an element of blues and noise into a band.

For years to come, Brannon would faithfully attend any

Nick Cave show he could. When Birthday Party disbanded that year, Brannon kept the faith, following any move the members made. He listened diligently to the entire Birthday Party catalog, which Strickland curated in a typically tasteful record collection. The two of them shared the love of this new, artistically original mass of sound.

But Brannon was careful enough, and creative enough, to never ape, copy, or mimic.

"You can like a band or a sound without sounding like it," Brannon told friends.

But you could use it, he added, as inspiration.

Which is what he planned to do even as he continued with Negative Approach.

This band has run its course, he thought at one point. *Something's going to change.*

Mike Danner had for years watched Brannon and Strickland from afar.

He was from suburban Milford, the son of a graphic designer dad and an arts-tilted mom whose love of music rubbed off quickly on her son, the oldest of two boys. She listened to a lot of funk, part of the region's musical terrain fed by Motown and nurtured by Westbound Records' Funkadelic.

Danner chose drums, the toys that make the noise. Before long, he was digging into a wilder strain of local music that led him to the hardcore scene led by Negative Approach and a cadre of like-minded musical anarchists, including Strickland.

"I met them first as a fan," Danner says, a by-product of hitting every Detroit show he could. He was drawn by both the scene and the music, and he'd been awed by Brannon.

When Danner began playing in a couple of local hardcore bands, he became a peer of the Negative Approach orbit. One of his bands practiced in the same space in Cass Corridor. And Danner was good.

"I started hanging out with them," Danner says. "They would play records for me that I never would've been turned on to, like Alice Cooper, all this glam rock stuff, the [New York] Dolls."

He started a band with Strickland, Eleventh Episode, with her on bass. They practiced and wrote songs during the summer of 1983, the impact of the Birthday Party's show still fresh, but never played a show.

Brannon, meantime, was still trying to hold Negative Approach together.

The band was preparing to record its first full-length record, *Tied Down*, which would coalesce the band's two-year reign of hardcore mastery in the Motor City.

Negative Approach was getting together every few nights to rehearse the ten new songs that would be *Tied Down*.

"But we were all living these separate lives by now," says NA guitarist Rob McCullough, whose brother, Graham, was NA's bassist. "Being so young, that meant a lot. We still had the music in mind that we wanted to do, but there was also part of us that wanted to do something more. And John didn't like that."

Add to that a twisted Yoko factor: Strickland was turning into a regular heroin user, while Brannon was a committed drinker and drugger. The McCulloughs and drummer Chris Moore were straight.

Strickland's habit and sometimes surly disposition turned into a problem for the rest of the band.

"She was difficult. She would try to tell us what to do, and more often, try to tell John what to do," Moore says.

Tied Down came out on Touch and Go in 1983. The fragmented band did some live dates and broke up mid-tour in Memphis.

While Brannon was gone, trying to milk the last drops of hardcore out of his band, Nick Cave came back to Detroit with his new band, the Bad Seeds, to support their debut album, *From Her to Eternity*.

Cave's destination that night?

"He stayed at my place at Cass and Willis in the [Cass] Corridor," Brannon says.

"Larissa totally hooked him up, you know, she scored for him."

The Bad Seeds tour had started in New York a week earlier, and while the shows were solid, Cave "had quite a bad habit; it was really out of control," said tour manager Jessamy Calkin.

"He ended up hanging out with Scott [Schuer, L-Seven guitarist] and Larissa," says Dave Rice, guitarist and one of the original L-Seven members. "Scott was driving Nick Cave around looking to score, and Cave was searching under the seats. Scott had a seventies Impala and Scott's like, 'What are you looking for?' And Cave says, 'Where's your shotgun? Doesn't everybody in Detroit have a shotgun?'"

Cave and Strickland came back to the Clubhouse to get high.

"Your boyfriend won't mind I'm here?" Cave asked.

"Oh, he's cool," Strickland said. "He'll get a kick out of knowing that you were here."

Cave, stoned and satisfied, went through their impressive record collection, pulling records out and placing them in stacks.

The good stuff went to one pile, including the Stooges, Alice Cooper, and Amboy Dukes, while the records he didn't like went in the other stack, which included all the Bowie records.

"She said he was the coolest dude," Brannon says.

Negative Approach was done, the victim of Nick Cave, the Birthday Party, and the blues. No more slam-dance soirees playing for groups of mostly male leather-jacketed meanies.

"I knew I was going to do something new," Brannon says. "Even as we broke up, that's where my head was at. Hardcore was, for me, over."

After their gear was ripped off for the third time from their Cass Avenue dive, he and Strickland began to squat at the Women's City Club, taking up the sixth floor of the ten-story building just off Woodward, the city's main drag.

Downstairs was a live music venue that hosted national touring bands. But the crime element, part of the fabric of Detroit, was always festering.

"The building had like, you know, [street gang] Pony Down living there, and Young Boys Incorporated," says Brannon, who was surviving on welfare in a state that had a 16 percent unemployment rate in the early eighties. "We were living upstairs while the touring bands played in this big room downstairs on the second floor."

Brannon and Strickland were the lords of the Detroit hardcore scene and people came over to listen to music and learn. That music was not just hardcore, though, and the growing influence and love of slower, darker, bluesier music was making the playlist. Brannon one night walked a couple of miles to the Soup Kitchen Saloon to see John Lee Hooker. "I got his autograph," Brannon says.

Through their diligent, reverent music consumption, and helped along by Brannon's admiration for Cave and the blues, they began to realize that they could form a band that would incorporate those influences. Brannon was learning guitar, Strickland could play bass, and Danner, who had moved from fanboy admirer to trusted friend, was a solid drummer.

Fed up with the sketch of Detroit, Brannon and Strickland loaded up Brannon's new Dodge Ram van, a gift from his father. It easily held everything they owned—two suitcases of clothes, numerous stacks of records, a 1972 Stratocaster, and a Fender Twin Reverb amp. They headed west, out of Detroit, forty-five miles to Ann Arbor.

Rent there was cheap, it was relatively safe, and it was the hometown of two of Brannon's favorite bands: the Stooges and MC5.

Danner, who had been making twelve dollars an hour at a machine shop in Detroit—a fortune in recession-ravaged Michigan—joined them.

The jobless trio lived in the van for three weeks, cleaning up in rest area washrooms, then moving to a series of houses, student living places, one a little away from the town and another a summer rental space in the student ghetto of the University of Michigan.

Danner and Brannon got jobs at Harry's Army Surplus, an Ann Arbor fixture since 1950. Strickland found work at Middle Earth, a mom-and-pop-owned trinket retailer that sold jewelry, folk art, postcards, and candles.

What they needed now was a guitarist. Danner had an idea.

●

Like Brannon, Strickland, and Danner, Kevin Monroe had moved from Detroit to Ann Arbor. His pursuit was romance rather than music; his girlfriend at the time went to school in Ann Arbor. Monroe wanted to play in a band but was working temp gigs through Manpower and driving a cab while practicing his guitar chops with no one to trade licks with.

Locals saw him on occasion hitchhiking, a real throwback in 1986, his cropped crew cut and eccentric clothing making him stand out even in the progressive headquarters of a prominent college town.

"I'd known John and Larissa when they lived at the City Club, but not well," Monroe says. "They were intimidating."

Danner, though, knew Monroe; his current girlfriend was besties with Monroe's paramour. And when conversation at the house turned to finding a guitarist, he suggested Monroe.

"I know this dude who can jam," Danner said one night as the three talked. "His name is Kevin," he said, "and he plays guitar."

When Monroe came over and plugged in his guitar, he could play a credible version of AC/DC's "Hells Bells."

"I'm like, 'All right, this is a start, dude,'" Brannon says. "You can go from here to there, so you know, Kevin just kind of came up and him and Larissa learned how to play from scratch together."

It was how Brannon envisioned it: a troop that was well versed in good music forming a band "out of nothing."

"I wanted to get these guys who are not affected by everything. When we all hung out and partied, we all kind of dug the same bands. So we were all on the same vibe."

It was what he needed to make "the greatest band in the world."

The tryout went well, and Monroe was invited to join, but there was an issue: Brannon and Strickland wanted to make sure their sound remained intact. If Monroe was the guitarist and left, it would create a gap in their songs, as guitarists vary widely in their approach, and few want to ape the approach of their predecessor.

How about if Strickland moved to guitar and Monroe take bass? Monroe agreed. For him, it was an honor to be asked to play with them.

He set about making himself irreplaceable, creating bass lines fashioned out of guitar riffs. "This was something that I really wanted to do, and I was nervous at first about getting kicked out," he says.

They had no bitches with his approach to the instrument. But the clothes . . .

Brannon and Strickland were put off by Monroe's fashion sense. They already had a no-shorts rule, part of a strict policy about appearances.

"You need to say something to him," Brannon, who didn't like confrontation, told Strickland. She was more than willing to give an order.

Monroe enjoyed a street style of dress and that included sometimes dressing like a British Oi boy, complete with braces and boots.

"It's a uniform," Strickland said to him.

"It's not a uniform; I'm not in any club," Monroe responded.

Her suggestion was to dig more into his own thing. Strickland wanted to ensure any kind of look didn't get misconstrued, as the Oi movement was often mistakenly perceived as having racist roots.

"They weren't trying to insult me," Monroe says. But he took her advice.

Monroe moved in with the band. He grew a beard, which came in full and red and was, for the time, outlandish. He donned a suit jacket, and sometimes wore a Lincoln-style top hat. He developed his own look, and the band had a striking visual even before its sound was realized.

"They wanted a commitment, financially and emotionally," Monroe says.

Soon, they moved to what would be the Hyena house, which would be their headquarters for five years, at 3416 Platt Road in Ann Arbor. It was a small brownstone on a corner lot that packed five bedrooms and two bathrooms into barely 1,200 square feet. The big draw was the basement, which was two rooms and provided a large practice space. While some basements were cubby holes where bands practiced on top of each other—amps tilted inward to make up for the lack of monitors—this space allowed them to set up as if playing from a stage, with plenty of room for everyone.

Brannon and Strickland now had an unnamed band with which they would wage war on tradition.

Ann Arbor was the perfect refuge for artistic deviants and muckrakers, with its history of rebellious culture. It was the home of the University of Michigan, a land-grant public university that opened in 1841 with a class of seven students and had grown to stake a claim to being a premier Midwestern school.

The town grew up around the school and had become synonymous with the high-minded academic reputation of U of M, which prided itself on its exclusivity and national stature. When the Vietnam War protests erupted in the sixties, the school, like so many others, was a hotbed of radicalism and upheaval. Fleecy-haired young men and their granny-glasses-and-sandals girlfriends rallied against The Establishment. The protests, rarely violent but often loud, bled into the community at large, creating a town of wild-minded, idealistic radicals.

Bands flocked to the town after the Detroit riots of 1967, enamored of the wider spaces that allowed for sprawling compounds where they could rehearse any time without worry of bitching neighbors or thieving interlopers.

When sixties band SRC scored a big advance from Capitol Records, they ploughed the money into a farmhouse and built a studio in Ann Arbor. Ted Nugent lived in an apartment in the middle of the student ghetto for a time as he broke in some new Amboy Dukes. All the four Stooges were raised in Ann Arbor, and MC5 moved there to join the club, escaping Detroit the same as Brannon and Strickland did.

"Things got too dangerous in Detroit," MC5 guitarist Wayne Kramer told this author in 2010. "Our gear got ripped off twice."

MC5 drummer Dennis Thompson explained, also to this author, that the band house on Hill Street was the hub of radical activity in the late sixties.

"The Ann Arbor house was the house where everybody came through," Thompson said. "People like the Sun Ra Arkestra and undercover feds and Black Panthers. The lieutenant of the [local] narcotics division used to come once a month just to make sure we weren't running drugs and dope."

Pioneer High School, adjacent to the University of

Michigan's fabled football stadium, graduated some of the most influential musicians in the advent of rock 'n' roll, including Ron and Scott Asheton of the Stooges, Bob Seger, and Iggy Pop.

The town of one hundred thousand people was steeped in a musical history that inspired legions of like-minded dreamers. The Hyenas were the newest of those aspirants, unformed but ready to take in the vibe.

"It was a town full of our influences," Brannon says. "This was the place we wanted to be to make this happen."

The band would be the Laughing Hyenas, taken from the members sitting around watching a Lorne Greene–hosted TV show on animals, *Lorne Greene's New Wilderness.*

Despite their relative newness to playing, they were devoted musicians.

"We practiced for hours almost every day," Danner recalls. It was a military-styled execution: writing songs, editing them, and then tossing them aside.

"We were overly critical of our sounds," Danner says. "We had grown up listening to glam rock and hardcore, and the sound we had was far from hardcore. We didn't want even a speck of evidence of our influences in our music. So it was impossible to write a song influenced by people that we loved and listened to but without ripping them off. So we threw away ten times more songs than we kept."

Strickland's guitar playing was limited by her newness to the instrument. She played riffs, simple-three note phrases, as she learned the fretboard.

"Larissa just picked up guitar with an approach of just knowing what she liked," Monroe says. "So she came up with her own sort of approach and so did I."

The house on Platt was where Brannon's "Monkee's vision" came together, based on the sixties TV show. Everyone living in the same house, practicing every day, working out songs, coming up with what could be the successor to hardcore—another underground lifeline for people who just didn't see things the way most people did.

The songs came slowly. Many were clearly influenced by the Birthday Party, with extended bass riffs, angular guitar, and Brannon's guttural grunts over the top.

It was work. They executed with diligence and enjoyed the art of art, of creating and trying to accomplish something.

Meanwhile, a bonus of the move to Ann Arbor was the company they kept.

"One night, I'm walking down the street going to the party store and I hear this band playing, coming out of a basement," Brannon says. "I'm like, 'Damn, that sounds like Ron Asheton.' I come back another time, again, 'Damn, that sounds like Ron Asheton.'"

It was.

A few houses down, Asheton's band Destroy All Monsters was rehearsing in the rental home of Michael Davis, the former bassist from MC5.

The band was better known for its members than its sound, which featured a monotone-voiced singer named Niagara backed by a pseudo-psychedelic foursome that included the former Stooge Asheton along with Davis.

They'd released a single in 1977 with the hopes of keeping alive the Ann Arbor tradition of musical importance.

Instead, Destroy All Monsters churned out losing propositions that no one outside Michigan dug. While the Hyenas were the new kids and full of energized creativity, the

Destroy All Monsters camp "just wanted to drink beer and smoke cigarettes and play," says David Keeps, who managed the band for several years. "I mean, they were creative, and they wrote songs and stuff like that. But in general, they were just regular Joe musicians and that's what they wanted to do."

Brannon, never shy about approaching his musical heroes, knocked on the door and introduced himself.

"I ended up becoming great friends with Michael Davis," Brannon says. "He started coming over to our house and hanging out."

Both Ashetons, Ron and his brother, Scott, also visited, drinking beer and listening to whatever Strickland put on the turntable. The Scientists, the Birthday Party, Coltrane, and Miles were all fixtures in the house. They spent days smoking weed, digging the sounds, then, once guests left, the band was back in the basement, adding some 40-ouncers to the mix.

The first Laughing Hyenas show was April 10, 1985, at Joe's Star Lounge in Ann Arbor, opening for Destroy All Monsters. The venue was an established part of Ann Arbor's music scene, hosting pre-fame Replacements and Violent Femmes, hardcore matinees, and noise bands. Negative Approach had played there, as had Destroy All Monsters.

The night before was a show by Love Tractor, an inoffensive Athens, Georgia–based folk-pop foursome. A month before, Gil Scott-Heron had played Joe's. The bookings were wide open.

For the Hyenas, the Wednesday night opening spot was a gift. A hometown debut with a set of the six originals they had drummed up. Most of the songs they played would soon be discarded, including "Red Hour," a song based on a *Star Trek* episode.

The show went like a first show should; it wasn't a victory but certainly not a disaster, as Brannon and Strickland had considerable stage experience. The sound was balanced; the songs were relatively tight.

"How'd that sound?" Monroe asked Davis after the sparsely attended set.

"It was okay," Davis responded, out of kindness. As a veteran, he could see the rough spots.

The Hyenas headed back to the basement. In two weeks, they were opening for Die Kreuzen, a Milwaukee hardcore band, as well as LA-based Minutemen at Traxx in Detroit.

The rehearsals ratcheted up, but new songs were slow in coming. Everything took a long time, as they were perfectionists. And there was a social whirl being in Ann Arbor that took up some of their time. In addition to their neighbors, Destroy All Monsters, the town still hopped with some of the same counterculture revolution it was known for, which meant plenty of parties and shows.

The Hyenas were eagerly joining a fraternity, and they fit right in. "Flyering," a now extinct practice of putting up posters advertising an upcoming show in record stores and head shops and on streetlight posts and telephone poles was the internet posting of its time.

Brannon loved taking handfuls of flyers and a staple gun and heading out into the town, meeting people and inviting them to the next Hyenas show.

"We'd pass out flyers at the gigs," Brannon says. "All this shit was word of mouth. No internet. No MTV. No radio play. Everything was done with cassette tapes and letters, so you're talking about creating something out of nothing."

He and Strickland got tighter as a couple. He began to join her in sharing drugs, along with emotions. She became vigilant over Brannon, a power couple of excess.

One night the band drove down to Detroit to see Screaming Jay Hawkins at the Soup Kitchen Saloon, where Brannon had seen John Lee Hooker a couple of years earlier, a blues room that legally held 130 or so people but would pack out at 200 elbow to elbow. Willie Dixon, Luther Allison, and Jimmy Rogers all played the downtown joint at some point, situated two blocks from the Detroit River.

Everyone got drunk, and the drive back to Platt Road was a hairy episode. When they stumbled out of the van, Brannon made it to the back steps but fell into the bushes.

"You guys need to watch out for him," Strickland screamed at Danner and Monroe, who could barely watch out for themselves, as she helped Brannon to his feet.

Danner recalls now that "it was clear they were the two in this that needed to be protected. But John needed more protecting, and that was what Larissa did."

The show with the Minutemen went a little better than the one at Joe's, the reaction more enthusiastic. They did the same set as at Joe's. Danner was keeping the songs tribal, with few frills and a steady two-tub beat, ignoring the snare whenever possible. The only song that was fully formed was "Soul Kiss." A chord change that would become part of "Playground" popped in and out as well.

The Minutemen came back to the house after the show and got a lesson in beer hoarding, a Midwest tradition.

The band hung out, drank beer, and ate cold artichokes in the kitchen with everyone. When the after-party wound down, the Minutemen, being polite guests, gathered the empty beer bottles to put them back in the case, and noticed six were missing. Where were they?

"Check the vegetable crisper," someone local said.

Sure enough, three bottles of beer. The other three bottles were found years later in the drawer of an unused desk in the kitchen. These were stashed by Brannon just in case the beer ran out someday in the future.

Then it was back to the basement. They had a series of shows scheduled for the summer of 1985 at Graystone Hall, a former movie theater that opened in the thirties. It was in one more crappy part of Detroit and drew little attention from the cops. The owner was Russ Gibb, the man who founded the Grande Ballroom, an iconic club of the sixties that broke MC5 and the Stooges, and hosted everyone from the Who to Cream to Led Zeppelin.

The best part for the kids is that it was booked and operated by Rusk, the Touch and Go Records chief, and therefore had a rotating cast of primo bands from his label.

"Russ ended up buying the Graystone, and the agreement was that he would put up the money and buy the building and he would buy a PA," Rusk says. "I would agree that I was gonna run the place and do whatever the fuck it took to make it work, and that he wasn't going to put in any money beyond that."

Rusk had put out records by Negative Approach and L-Seven and liked Brannon and Strickland. But he wasn't impressed with the new, unformed Hyenas.

"It wasn't something [good] right off the bat," Rusk says.

The Hyenas played more shows in 1985, including a gig at the W.J. Maxey Boys Training School, a sixty-inmate juvenile detention facility outside Jackson, Michigan.

They kept landing good shows. In early 1986, the Hyenas

opened for the Butthole Surfers, Sonic Youth, and Swans in separate Detroit shows.

The songs that would be on the first Hyenas record, the EP *Merry Go Round*, took shape. "I wrote 'Stain' early, along with 'That Girl'; those were the first songs," Brannon says. "And at that point, I was playing guitar, but I never actually played it live. I would come up with the riff and was sure somebody could play it better. I was playing a lot, like I had a bass guitar too, and I was hanging out with Larissa listening to Joy Division. I kept trying to come up with a cool bass line. Then I wrote 'Hell's Kitchen'; that's Kevin's bass line. Everyone was starting to learn how to play, and Kevin always had a great sense of music."

The lyrics dealt with criminals, Jim Thompson–esque bad girls and weapons. The songs became more traditional than their earlier works, less chaotic with clearly defined changes. One song, "Gabriel," had a trumpet on it.

John Brannon playing with the band in 1987 at the Intersection in Grand Rapids, Michigan. Photo by Jon Howard.

"The first thing that ever hit me before I knew about rock 'n' roll was Louis Armstrong on TV," Brannon says. He played trumpet as an elementary school kid because "that just spoke to me."

A lot of the songs started with Monroe's bass blasting away, backed by Danner's subdued, tom-heavy beats. There were no individual credits or publishing issues. The consideration was absurd.

They'd recorded themselves on portable cassettes to hone their songs, but now they felt ready to record a demo.

Rusk had come by early on with a cassette recorder, let them play, and considered the results. "He was doing it as a favor," Brannon says. "We were friends, and he wanted to give us a chance. But we weren't ready at all."

Some of the songs, including an early dirge called "Chuck's Jism," were scrapped shortly after being recorded.

"You guys need to practice," Rusk told Brannon.

It was a blow, but "we just got down to practicing more," Brannon says.

While searching for a label, the band kept hammering away at their songs, tweaking things. A practice session was also a dry run for a live show, and they were as interested in presentation as they were sound.

Not long after the Rusk tapes, Monroe trash-picked a four-track cassette recorder. They found some microphones and recorded themselves, this time with several months of practice and songs that had become fully realized.

The results were much better. Their sound was more developed. Songs had starts and stops, and the band members were tight from constant practice.

The session became a self-released cassette that made the rounds among traders and music fans. The crude black-

and-white paper sleeve, featuring a wheelie-popping hot rod on the cover and murky photos of the band inside, was produced in haste. This wasn't an official release; it was just a taste. Yet it got the band its first rave review, from *Creem* magazine no less.

"It took 16 years, but Ann Arbor has finally produced a recording that can serve as the natural follow-up/extension to the Stooges' *Fun House*," the review read. "These six incredible terror tunes embody chaos, fear, pain, love, hate, desire to maim, you name it."

More attention and more gigs came with the tape. The Hyenas became even more ambitious.

But before anything, they'd have to find a new drummer because Danner quit. He insists that things weren't moving fast enough.

"I don't really know what it was," Danner says. "I needed more."

He'd already moved out of the house on Platt to stay with a girl he'd met in Ann Arbor.

"It was so much nicer than our house," he says. "And it took me out of the mix of our little family, living together and jamming together. I just kind of drifted away."

Brannon says it was his and Strickland's ambition that drove Danner away.

"At this point, it was 'Hey, Mike, all right, we're making these recordings, you know we're taking this shit on the road.' He probably wasn't cut out for it at that point."

Monroe contends it was Strickland that made Danner leave.

"He couldn't deal with Larissa," he says. Strickland was

dramatic, controlling, and addicted. She'd been a user for a few years already, and Brannon was also into it. Ann Arbor was also a main connection for dealers running between Detroit and Chicago down Interstate 94.

"As soon as we moved to Ann Arbor, that's when the horse kicked in," Brannon says.

Strickland's difficult nature would become a common problem, as her immense creativity was fueled in part by her habits, which would make her too difficult for most people, as it turned out.

SIDE 2

"Wanted: punk blues drummer."

The to-the-point, letter-sized ad was posted at Schoolkids Records in Ann Arbor, with, optimistically, ten tear tabs at the bottom with the phone number of the Platt Road house.

Jim Kimball was an Ann Arbor native and the only person to respond.

While the other members of the Laughing Hyenas were Ann Arbor outsiders, Kimball was a local hero, mostly by virtue of his father's legend as a diving coach at the University of Michigan.

Jim Kimball turned twenty in the summer of 1986 and only two years before had landed in the pages of the *Ann Arbor News*, feted for "best percussion" in a high school jazz festival. The photo of the winners includes Kimball sporting an amused half smile, bushy eyebrows, and a wispy moustache.

As a kid, Kimball was groomed as a diver, following the lead of his older brother and sister. But he first wanted to be a professional football player when he grew up before aiming at a life as a rock star. He was ten years old when he told his mom he had no interest in sports as a career.

Drumming was his passion. She told him if that was his choice, he had to listen to jazz as well as the rock 'n' roll he was already following.

She played him some Billie Holiday and Dinah Washington. He took it from there, following Buddy Rich, seeing him twice when the legendary drummer came to play Ann Arbor. Kimball began a subscription to *Modern Drummer* magazine that lasted twenty years. His inspirations were Rich, Keith Moon, and Mitch Mitchell.

By the time he was in junior high, he'd played in school combos that performed at Crisler Arena, a thirteen thousand–capacity stadium that is home to U of M's basketball team

"We did 'Hawaii Five-O,' 'Aquarius [Let the Sunshine In],' and 'Wipe Out' with horns and everything," Kimball says. He was fourteen years old.

At the time he saw the Hyenas ad in the record store, Kimball was playing in a new wave band called Surreal Estate, a three-piece that had a self-released record out. The back cover shows Kimball in a suit jacket and tie, and the Thanks list includes his parents, Dick and Gail Kimball; they'd funded the studio time for the platter.

He came to Platt Road without his drums to first meet everyone. It was uncomfortable, as the three Hyenas had already formed a team. They had a look: Brannon in blue-collar work shirts, baggy Dickies pants, and boots, while Strickland stuck with the dime-store fashions, girlie and feminine despite her aggressive nature. Monroe was, to Kimball's eyes, a weirdo.

Kimball was still an innocent, a natural athlete in good shape and clad in jeans and a polo shirt.

"I was totally different from them in every way," Kimball says. His listening included timid pop bands like the Police and other tame eighties new wave. His aggro music exposure was limited to the Ramones. He had never heard of Negative Approach let alone John Brannon or hardcore punk rock.

But the trio of sketchy Detroiters seemed committed, and Kimball was up for a life in music.

John Brannon in the house on Platt Road. Photo by Kevin Monroe.

"Here's a tape of the songs," Brannon said after the four had talked a little bit in the living room. "Check this out for a couple days and we'll jam."

Kimball came back with his drums, set up in the basement, and had learned the songs already.

So they threw him a curve.

"Play 'So What' by Miles Davis," Brannon said, trying to find a flaw. He knew of Kimball's jazz background, but even with that, the modal jazz tune off 1959's *Kind of Blue* LP was surely a challenge.

It wasn't.

With a style leaning into precision rather than vigor, Kimball initially didn't hit hard enough to break through the wall of bass and guitar much less Brannon's howl.

But Kimball wanted the gig and knew what was needed. He could do the blues, he could play mid-tempo jazz, and he could, with some practice, master the tribal pounding of the songs on the tape Brannon had given him.

"Hit harder" became a mantra over the next few days and the drummer delivered with gusto. They had long rehearsals and Kimball stayed on top of the songs, each take getting stronger, with louder thuds.

He left after the second day and the three convened.

"We're like, 'All right, we're living here, we don't know anybody,'" Brannon says. They realized the slim pickings in the college town for anyone willing to play their music and put up with them. And Kimball was eager.

"We thought, 'This dude can learn to hit hard, man; plus he's got swing,'" Brannon says.

Kimball had played himself into the band, switching out his 7A sticks, lightweight with tips, for double-butted sticks with no tips. Using his athletic learnings, he willed himself to pound, creating a heavy rhythm while maintaining control.

Kind of.

Kimball moved into the band house, taking a bedroom with his collie retriever, Salvador. He quickly realized that the Laughing Hyenas were no democracy. This was a vision as much as it was a band.

"Larissa and I had nothing else beyond rock 'n' roll," Brannon says. "We were so driven to do this. And it's like, I had to deal with what I had to deal with in Negative

Approach and with high school kids. So you know some members were doing this as a hobby, but at this point, with the Hyenas, I'm in full force. This is what I'm doing. This is a make-or-break situation."

Every band needs a dictator of some shape or form. Democratic bands—"Is this OK?"—often fall prey to mediocrity. A vision is needed; there's a reason Jagger/Richards and Page/Plant are the rule, a dynamic duo (or an individual) with a mission and a vision.

Muses vary, but oversight and a take-charge dynamic are necessary. Mark E. Smith shared songwriting credits freely but controlled the revolving cast that was the Fall all the way down to what was played on the cassette player in the van or, later, on the bus. John Lydon hired and fired at will for a long time as he converted his creativity to reality after the Sex Pistols and Public Image Mach 1. Tom Verlaine in Television insisted on writing and arranging everything. The list of great musical authoritarians is long.

In the case of the Hyenas, it was Brannon and Strickland who ruled, and then some.

They're incredibly controlling, Kimball thought after a few rehearsals.

The band meetings Strickland called sometimes consisted of "me and Kevin sitting there listening to her complain about . . . anything," he says. "We'd all meet in the living room for a three-hour lecture from Larissa."

It took a couple of months to get Kimball into Hyenas-level playing shape, and everyone kept a schedule: work, rehearse, socialize, sleep, repeat. Kimball learned the songs from the demo, adding his growing power to the tunes.

They worked their jobs: Kimball at Uno's, a pizza place; Brannon hanging in at the military surplus store; and

Strickland at Middle Earth, the home goods place.

Monroe relished his gig as a cab driver, fancying himself a college town Travis Bickle, watching the street life. "It was like being a cop in that you see this underbelly of society in such a way," Monroe says. "At first it was exciting. I could come and go as I wanted. But as far as money, it was more of an adventure than a job."

They ate when they could afford to or when Kimball brought home leftover pizzas. Brannon dumpster dived. No one had much money, but they didn't need it. They were working at their art, almost every night, to create something to inflict on the world.

They were still learning dynamics, practicing slow builds, and making sure their breaks were tight.

"That was the wonderful thing about living in a house as a band; you can really accomplish stuff that way," says Monroe.

The well-received demo was helping them land local gigs, but they needed to get something out more broadly in order to tour. Rather than take the demo to Rusk, though, Brannon and the rest wondered if there were other labels that might be interested. They were stung by Rusk's initial dismissal.

In 1987, MTV was raging, and mainstream mediocrity was the flavor on even the margins of the music industry. If the clear-headed Rusk didn't see their appeal, who would?

Peach of Immortality was among the better of noisy industrial bands making their way in and around the music underground. The project was led by Tom Smith, an instigator, mischief-maker, and high creative. He came to Brannon's attention when Negative Approach played in Washington, DC, and Smith's record label, Adult Contemporary Recordings, came up in a conversation with members of Pussy Galore, major players in the East Coast noise/rock scene.

Smith was a Georgia native who had recently moved to DC. His claim to fame was that he was in a pre-R.E.M. band with a green-haired Michael Stipe, Boat Of.

Larissa Strickland, Jim Kimball, Kevin Monroe, John Brannon in Ypsilanti, Michigan, 1987. Photo by C.M. Linabury. Courtesy of John Brannon.

Adult Contemporary Recordings was mostly vanity— all four of Peach of Immortality's LPs were on it—but Smith had also released an obsessed-with-obscurity three-song cassette by Pussy Galore. It was limited to ten copies, distributed through fanzine *Forced Exposure*.

Smith and his label were picked by Strickland as a potential home for the Hyenas proposed six-song EP.

"It went back and forth, and [Smith] wanted to do it, said he would do it, so we sent the tape and the artwork for the record to him in Washington, DC," Monroe says.

Where it languished. Print ads came out, indicating the Hyenas EP was forthcoming as Adult Contemporary release #11, just after a Drunks with Guns LP and before a Wishes and Water / Terveet Kädet split ten-inch.

None of the schedule was ever released. Drunks with Guns got a $500 advance from Smith in a check that the band later claimed bounced.

The Hyenas quest to get something released was iced. Smith didn't return their calls.

In an interview at the Ann Arbor radio station WCBN in June 1987, the band told listeners that it might be a while before the vinyl was released. Was anyone interested in helping them?

"We just wanna put it out the quickest way we can," Monroe said.

"Any donations are accepted, cash preferably," Strickland added.

A trip to Washington, DC, in July to play DC Space was the farthest the band had traveled for a show, opening for Ignition, a band fronted by Alec MacKaye, whose brother, Ian, was vocalist for the revered Minor Threat. He was just putting together his next band, Fugazi.

The show went well, with the Hyenas' Beltway debut readily accepted by an audience that was still half-footed in hardcore. The other half, though, was open-minded in a town where the Birthday Party—still an overt and recognizable influence for the Hyenas—had played its last US show ever in 1983.

The band stayed at MacKaye's parents' regal Georgetown

home, where Kimball, oblivious, fired up a joint.

"These guys created straight edge, so can you cool it with that shit?" Brannon ordered, always conscious of social constructs that had been erected in the vestiges of punk rock.

A month later, Alec MacKaye came to Ann Arbor as he was riding across the US on his motorcycle, visiting friends and taking in the country.

He was on his way to Chicago, where Touch and Go Records chief Corey Rusk had moved, seeking a bigger city and a new home to headquarter his expanding record label.

"We still have this tape, man, check it out," Brannon said to MacKaye. "Take a copy with you."

When he got to Chicago, MacKaye played the demo for Rusk.

This is not the same band, Rusk thought. He'd heard the tape before, but it landed differently this time. He called Brannon.

"The songs are great, but they need to be recorded better," Rusk told him. And he knew just the place to do it.

"I just did a record with Killdozer, from Wisconsin," Rusk told him. "And they recorded in Madison with a guy named Butch Vig. I'd like to get you there and record this."

Vig was a native of small-town Wisconsin, the son of a doctor, who, like thirty thousand other kids, headed to the University of Wisconsin at Madison in the early seventies, trying to figure out what was next.

Vig's love was music, having played the drums since he was a boy.

He opened Smart Studios in an old manufacturing building in 1983 with fellow student Steve Marker. The structure was two miles north of campus in an artists' desert. They had a thousand square feet to work with.

Vig and Marker's aim was to have a place for local bands to record at a reasonable price. Other studios were charging seventy-five dollars an hour for twenty-four tracks. Most of the local indie bands didn't have that kind of money, nor did they have much use for twenty-four tracks.

Smart Studios offered eight tracks for fifteen dollars an hour.

"We were the cheapest option out there," Vig says. "We could do these fast budget sessions."

Among their first clients was Killdozer, a Madison-based trio that onlookers lazily described as a blend of Flipper and the Birthday Party. The band recorded a twenty-one-minute EP at Smart in the fall of 1983 that was initially released by a small local label.

Touch and Go Records chief Rusk loved the humor and the sludgy sound of the EP and snapped it up, reissuing it on his label.

He added Killdozer to the roster, and they went back to Smart and Vig in March 1985. A full-length, *Snake Boy*, came out later in the year, again knocking Rusk out in both sound and price.

"After Killdozer, we got a lot of the Touch and Go bands," Vig says. "All because of Corey. He liked the price and the sound. We never had a contract. Then he told me, 'We've got this band, the Laughing Hyenas.' I'd never heard them."

The Hyenas jumped in the van and headed to Madison. For $1,203 in September 1987, they nailed seven tracks, plus $155 for four nights at the Red Roof Inn.

The songs included the six from the demo. Instead of rerecording "Soul Kiss," they put down "Candy."

The songs came to life in Vig's hands, with a brighter high end, a more pointed guitar sound, and bigger drums, all led by Monroe's punching, insistent bass.

"They loaded in their equipment and Larissa plugged her guitar, the Strat, into the Fender Twin and just turned it on ten," Vig says. "The fillings would fly out of your mouth."

While vocalists are usually isolated in a booth when recording, Vig put Strickland and her guitar rig in the booth instead.

After they'd loaded in, Brannon asked Vig if they could bring in their own PA.

"I had done that before but usually I just run the bass drum through it [for] more volume," Vig says. "But instead of doing that, they wanted to run everything through it to make it more live. And it wasn't a great-sounding PA, so that added to the sound."

Brannon was using a style he had read of the Stooges using when they recorded *Fun House* in 1970.

The PA was mic'ed, creating a split in the sound with both the board and the PA blending the sounds.

As a drummer, Vig added extra heft to the bass-heavy bottom of the band's sound.

"He made that Slingerland set of mine sound so good," Kimball says. "No one else ever could do that."

The songs were so tight, the band only needed two takes to nail them, max. One of the early Hyenas songs, "That Girl," was slowed down, making it the marquee tune from the collection.

Following the session, the Hyenas came back to Ann Arbor for a set at the Nectarine Ballroom to open for Hüsker Dü.

The Hyenas ripped through the new EP, and tossed in a few new songs, including "Love's My Only Crime," "Sister," and "Seven Come Eleven." All three were in full form, ready for release, but were not recorded on the first visit to Vig's.

About twenty-five minutes into the set, Brannon's mic gave out and the band jammed admirably while a tech grabbed a new one. They were taut and tight, so rehearsed that nothing could throw them.

Brannon drank from a pitcher of Budweiser, which he placed before the set on Monroe's bass cabinet like a sacrament; Kimball donned a black tie with a short-sleeved white button-up, looking like he would sell you a used Ford. Strickland's Twin Reverb sat on a milk crate; Kimball's kick drum was held in place by a cinder block.

Hüsker Dü was on Warner Bros. Records and arrived with sparkling flight cases for their instruments, a roadie, and a late-model van. If the Hyenas cared, the headlining group could have been a cautionary example; Hüsker Dü broke up a month later due to drummer Grant Hart's heroin addiction.

A month later, *Merry Go Round* began shipping. The not-so-simple indie-ness of the Hyenas cover art on the EP was starkly different from that of their corporate counterparts. It was developed by local music activist Tim Caldwell, who worked nights at a thermographic printshop. He was a known quantity, having had a hand in cover art for a single by Chicago band the Effigies.

"I wanted something cold and blown out with a carnival theme," Caldwell says.

The cover was shot by Rick Lieder, a local freelance photographer who had studied at the University of Michigan to become a physicist before he realized his love of art trumped a life of quantum gravity.

"I was a fan of local music and had been shooting bands," Lieder says. He had seen Negative Approach and became acquainted with Caldwell through a mutual interest in local science fiction clubs.

Caldwell took him over to the house on Platt Road to meet Brannon and Strickland, the first step for anyone working with the Hyenas.

"It was a very bare-bones house," Lieder says. "It was clear they didn't have a lot of money."

Brannon was loquacious, while Strickland listened.

"They both had their own ideas, and John was more animated," he says.

After reviewing some of his photo archive, Lieder presented shots he had taken on a visit to Disneyland in Anaheim, California, in 1984. He saw a little girl, maybe seven years old, on a carousal.

"I only took two pictures of her," Lieder says. But he never got a release signed, as he was still in the early stages of his career and never thought anything would come of the pictures.

It was immediately decided by Strickland that it would make a terrific cover image even with the girl cropped out, as was legally necessary. Despite the cropping, you can see four tiny fingers on the rail in the photo. The Hyenas paid Lieder $150 to use the picture.

The back image of the circus poster, Caldwell says, was taken "around Zug Island, where the MC5 and Leni [Sinclair, sixties photographer] shot famous pics of the group."

"Larissa and Kevin said to just make sure the Hyenas logo is up in marquee lights and credit the font to Gary Roscoe Johnson," a second-generation Detroit tattoo artist. "The red-and-black color scheme duotone wasn't a nod to Stendhal [author of the nineteenth-century novel *The Red and the Black*] but the colors most associated with lust and death that certain tunes covered," Caldwell says.

In the original photo, the colors are remarkably like what was used for the record cover, right down to the hue of red. The bulbs of the carousel are stark against the dark background, the little girl in her white dress with red trim looking away from the camera, unaware that her tiny hand would grace the cover of what would end up as a highly considered record.

Touch and Go pressed 2,715 vinyl copies and 906 cassettes of *Merry Go Round*.

The band members then threw a wrench into the credits. Both Larissa and Monroe took the last name "Strickland."

Larissa had to change her last name to protect her father; Nestor Stolarchuk's daughter was considered wayward in the Ukrainian community, a free spirit in a devout clan.

She and Brannon were driving one day past Strickland Market, a large convenience store, on the edge of downtown Ann Arbor.

"That's it," she said. "I'm going to call myself Strickland."

Monroe, though, contends they got it from the maiden name of his grandmother.

Either way, they borrowed something more than just a name. It was a way to mess with people.

"We liked the Butthole Surfers' thing about their drummers being siblings, so we decided to use 'Strickland' as a fake name and called each other brother and sister," Monroe says.

Interviewers and other strangers took it as fact, and the band would on occasion assert the fabrication.

The band wanted to create not just a sound but a mini culture of subversion, a twist on the Creepy Crawl, a Manson

Family trick of breaking into someone's home and altering it in some fashion, perhaps rearranging the furniture, leaving behind an uneasy reminder to the occupants upon their return.

Promotional sticker made by the band. Courtesy of Kevin Monroe.

Around Ann Arbor, stickers began to pop up, small at four by five inches, black-and-white, with short lines of text penned by Strickland or Monroe, usually with a Southern Gothic vibe.

The copy was informed by books donated to the Platt

house by Caldwell, including *Ol' Man Adam an' His Chillun* and *John Henry* by Roark Bradford, along with a batch of woodcuts.

The Hyenas were assisted in their stickers first by Danner, who worked in a printshop, then they carried on the practice after he left the band. It was an odd thing to see popping up, not just around Ann Arbor but wherever the band played, mostly Michigan in the beginning.

It was a smart, obscure strategy by an obscure band that was getting smarter.

By 1986, Touch and Go had blossomed into a full-fledged indie label that was putting out some of the best music in the US. Rusk was a credible, ambitious entrepreneur, always with an eye on finding something good to put out.

Rusk's handling of Touch and Go had been masterful. He'd parlayed a small DIY project into a revered independent record label, and sales were proving that he was also an adroit judge of talent.

"I signed bands that I liked," Rusk says. He did so on a handshake, unheard of for the most part even in the most remote of deals. No contracts.

Rusk's burgeoning empire was now run out of a wood-frame white house, in Chicago's North Park neighborhood, filled with workstations.

With a connection to one of the nation's hippest labels, the Hyenas kept a steady schedule of live dates, perfecting an explosive stage show.

"Larissa and I did the booking; she did a lot of the flyers," Monroe says. "We worked hard at it, collectively, to get as many dates as possible."

It was Strickland who collected the numbers and addresses of the venues, a treasure of contacts she had obtained from Black Flag back in 1981 when she met the band.

"Both John and Larissa really knew what they were doing in terms of making connections," says Bruce Adams, who worked with the band first as a roadie and merch guy and then later as a promotion manager at Touch and Go. "Larissa in particular knew how to organize a tour and book these dates."

Cleveland, Chicago, Pittsburgh, Cincinnati, Indianapolis, Columbus—the Midwest was jammed with venues ready to put the Hyenas on a bill. Mostly it was as an opener, since they had just the EP and some nascent underground cred compared to the heavier sway of local favorites and larger national acts. The Hyenas were regional, willing to play for whatever. They delivered every time.

"I think of their touring like a pebble hitting the pond, and the ripples moving out; this was how they did their live booking," Adams says.

Monroe tried his hand at the bookings as well.

"Larissa taught me a lot about booking bands," Monroe says. "But it was definitely a case of when we were starting out, we could handle it, we were doing as well as anyone could expect. There were some groups that could maintain that kind of thing, like Fugazi."

But bookings in those days were often fraught. A shady promoter would fail to come through with a paltry hundred-dollar guarantee, a hall would be shuttered, flyering would not get done.

"I booked a show at the Penguin pub in Youngstown, Ohio," Monroe says. "We got there and didn't have a gig. Something had fallen through. And I felt I had let the band down, even though it was only Youngstown."

Booking contracts were rare for upstart bands like the Hyenas and, as with the Touch and Go deal, trust was part of the deal. When a booking went wrong, there was no recompense. Sometimes trust didn't work.

Meanwhile, the house on Platt filled up with boxes of the new record and T-shirts, ready to drop into the van and boost their earnings on the road.

In between bookings, which were steadily picking up, the new songs were already working in the basement. "Sister" and "Lullaby and Good Night" were done, ready for the next record along with the three songs that they had finished before recording *Merry Go Round*.

The songs began to take on an identifiable sound, starting with Monroe's overdriven bass and Kimball's punching into the guitar, creating a throbbing wall of rhythm.

"It never started with Larissa," Kimball says. "It would be this bass/drum thing and then Larissa would talk with Kevin about what she was going to do. Some songs came quickly, some didn't. But no matter what, we'd play them over and over and over."

Most everyone wrote their own parts, Brannon coming in with lyrics last.

"I'm writing the bass riffs that were back and forth, repetitive," Monroe says. "It was influenced by blues stuff, but also Motown, soul, funk guys without being the Red Hot Chili Peppers."

Strickland came in with guitar riffs over the groove with an unschooled, sometimes atonal approach.

"No one ever told me what to do [on guitar]," Strickland

told an interviewer at the *Michigan Daily*, the student newspaper at the University of Michigan. "I've never had a teacher come in and say, 'No, that's not what you do.' I look at [it] as what I have in my head and what I think sounds good to me. So I looked at it in a totally naive way, and I think that helps the songwriting."

The live dates through the Midwest were broken up by longer spells in Ann Arbor, where they took shifts at their jobs, fielded visitors to the band house, and kept developing more songs.

"We were still very discerning as to where we would play," Monroe says. It wasn't even a year since the Detroit music scene had been a collective skeptic of the Hyenas.

But armed with the Touch and Go imprimatur, the Hyenas were becoming an item. They wanted to be the go-to for local promoters when larger bands came through, a reliable opener but a solid draw on their own. A $200 gig here, a $100 show there. Sometimes a local show would bring them more. House parties could pay $300 if you had someone honest on the door. Money was good, but it had become a crusade; cash was welcome, but they were going to do it anyway.

"Me and Larissa were just like 'Okay, we're just getting in the van and doing these gigs,'" Brannon says. "We didn't give a fuck about money."

SIDE 3

"I'm an adventurer," Hyenas bassist Kevin Monroe says. "I like adventure. I like music as an adventure and the drug thing was, like, an adventure for me. Historically I was into it, and I'm not afraid to do anything."

Strickland's heroin habit was well known to the street savvy, mysterious to the suburban kids who worshipped her and unknown to others, including drummer Jim Kimball, whose vices were limited to weed and booze.

Brannon had been doing dope off and on since he was a teenager. Together, the three formed a junkie alliance, a quiet but always present vibe that binds those in the know.

"I was as influential if not being more so, because of my personal connections there in Detroit and Ann Arbor," Monroe says. "Larissa didn't really introduce John to dope. But it didn't go crazy until we were all together. People might have tried one thing or another or been exposed to one pill or something else at a different time, but when we were all together in a band, everything was sort of keyed up in that direction."

Brannon said the drug habits blossomed in the house on Platt in Ann Arbor.

"Everybody had bad habits," he later said. "Heroin was my drug of choice. It just seemed like a good idea at the time. There were no underlying issues that led me to try it. I was young and dumb, and I wanted to experiment and get high. It was fun for the first three years I did it, and it was a nightmare for the rest of it. We just got caught up in that whole thing and it was really hard to quit. I gotta say, though, we were doing a lot of drugs, but it was the most prolific period we had."

To score, they would head back to the neighborhood they had left in Detroit.

"We were aware of all the dealers," Brannon says. "It might have been like a once-a-month thing for [Strickland] when we first got to Ann Arbor. It wasn't a daily thing at that point. Then, pretty soon, it became a regular thing."

Defying the concept of the "Just Say No" era, the band began 1988 keeping faithful to its goal of writing new songs and playing live dates while sticking with their menial jobs and obeying their habits.

It was early that year when former Negative Approach drummer Chris Moore suspected that the drug habit of Strickland had led to more consistent use by Brannon.

"We always stayed in touch, and when I went to see him in Ann Arbor, he was elusive and different; [you're] not sure who you're talking to at the time," says Moore, who was friends with both Brannon and Strickland.

The house on Platt Road became a destination for friends like Moore, who gathered in the living room to listen to whatever Brannon or Strickland wanted them to hear.

The vibe was hippie punk with a side of humor. One of their roommates kept her dead myna bird, named Basil Rathbone after the suave South African actor, in the refrigerator for some cryogenic symbolism.

"We'd go up there and party with 'em, you know, hang out," says Andy Wendler, guitarist in the Necros, a band that inspired Brannon's Negative Approach. The Necros had disbanded the previous year, but most members remained part of the region's music scene.

The house drew visitors from all over the Midwest, and included Corey Rusk, the head of Touch and Go, along with his wife and business partner Lisa. David Viecelli, also known as Boche, visited from Windsor, Ontario, a year before he founded the Billions Corporation, a talent agency that would go on to book several Touch and Go bands, including Jesus Lizard, Arcwelder, and the Mekons, although it never handled the Hyenas.

"We'd listen to music, or we'd get pizza and watch a movie like *The Godfather*," Monroe says. "We weren't isolationists at home. We were living, at some times, this very normal lifestyle."

Strickland invited friends from her job at Middle Earth, the Ann Arbor retailer, and her sister, Anna, also an artist, would drop in.

Being a rental house, the landlord had the option to sell the place and give the tenants a set amount of time to move out. One day, a prospective buyer came by to look the house over.

He declined to buy it but shared with Strickland an amusing anecdote on the owner's take on her ruffian tenants.

"She thinks you guys are a cult or something," he told her.

She shared his comment with the rest one evening during practice. They beamed like they'd been praised as dignitaries.

●

The band's first shows of 1988 were a pair of weekend dates with two Touch and Go labelmates—Milwaukee's Die Kreuzen, who were at the time finishing their third album, *Century Days*, with Butch Vig at a studio in Waukesha, Wisconsin, and headliner Killdozer, a Madison, Wisconsin–based band who were recording their fourth LP at Vig's Smart Studios in Madison.

The bands connected in Toronto at the Silver Dollar Room, an old blues joint/strip club built onto a hotel that had hosted Bob Dylan and Leonard Cohen since opening in the late fifties.

There was already a growing reverence for Touch and Go bands, and to get three together drew a capacity of 170 Canadians on a fifteen-degree Friday night.

Before the show, local photographer Rick McGinnis asked to shoot the bands, setting up a tarp with some lights in a corner of the club. McGinnis promised each band they could keep anything they wanted. All agreed.

"[The Hyenas] were, even more than the other two bands, a very insular unit," McGinnis says. "They kept to themselves, grouped themselves together on my white painter's tarp backdrop in a tight little bunch, Larissa smoking the whole time, John very much unwilling to put himself up front as the 'leader' of the group. It took a bit of effort to get him to stand where I knew there'd be some light. The most charismatic of the four was probably Larissa, who made the most effort to engage during the shoot."

McGinnis noticed something most everyone did about the Hyenas—they were a tribe of four. Even when Strickland was doing her social best, the band was quiet, almost standoffish, an anomaly in the friendly Midwest. Brannon pacified himself with beer, loads of it. Kimball smoked weed incessantly, while Monroe could watch and learn, rarely offering an insight to whatever he was observing.

Onstage, the band stationed themselves close together, partly a function of hearing each other in case a house soundman wasn't up to snuff with the monitors.

But you could also see they felt some comfort from proximity to each other in a protective pack.

The next night, Die Kreuzen and the Hyenas played Paychecks, a club in the bedraggled Hamtramck neighborhood of Detroit. The flyer for the show was designed by Strickland and featured a rear headshot silhouette of a guy who looked a lot like Brannon, tears trickling from his eye, and a few lines from "What Tomorrow Brings," a song off *Merry Go Round*.

The next few weeks were spent lining up dates for a minor tour of the East Coast. Even for a brief ten days on the road, it meant more phone calls, more mailing, more rehearsal, and more flyers. Most promoters would handle the promotion end, including the poster printing, which could be a substantial cost unless, like the Hyenas, you had a connection at the local printshop. Strickland often offered to design the flyer, have a few hundred printed locally by a connected friend, and ship them to the venue.

The band's first tour began ominously with a cancelled date in Chicago in mid-March. Bruce Adams, who volunteered to serve as roadie and to work the merchandise table to sell T-shirts and records, wrote a tour diary for the fanzine *Your Flesh*, a Minneapolis-based magazine whose publisher, Peter Davis, was a cranky, hyperliterate Californian transplant.

Davis had met Strickland when her band L-Seven

played the 7th St Entry in Minneapolis, opening a series of Midwestern dates with the Gun Club in summer of 1982.

"She was so connected, and she became a great pen pal," Davis says, referring to an old practice of exchanging letters sent via snail mail.

"The one thing she turned me on to is whatever Brannon was up to," Davis says. "She put [Negative Approach] on the map for me."

Strickland had a copy of the latest *Touch and Go* mag in her bag, "and it was the first time I saw that magazine . . . She was cool on that level."

Strickland was a sharp social maven, it appeared to Davis.

After the cancelled Chicago show, the band headed out on March 22, 1988, stopping in suburban Syracuse to stay at Adams's parents' house. The first show was the next night at T.T. the Bear's Place in Boston.

"We arrived at the club in Cambridge at 4:30 (as per promoter's suggestion) to be told that sound-check is at 7:30," Adams wrote in his diary. "Jim Kimball goes to the Boston Uno's to snag some free pizza."

Later: "The Hyenas rip into their set and Jim breaks his drum pedal on 'Playground.' He slams it back together . . . Along with 'Lullaby,' it makes an incredible one-two punch. The crowd seemed passive to me, just working it up. More people showed up to see headliners Pussy Galore."

The next night, the band played Maxwell's in Hoboken, New Jersey, an institution of such importance that Adams noted in his journal, "the Hyenas needed to be good." It was the band's New York area debut, a territory that Strickland knew well from her days attending Parsons School of Design.

The venue was a dark, moldy-smelling place that held two hundred but jammed in more fans for the biggest shows. A who's who of indie royalty played Maxwell's from Sonic Youth to Royal Trux to Redd Kross. Bands that made good there were rewarded with coolness points and some good-mouthing among tastemakers.

The Hyenas rose to the occasion. "Very good," Adams noted in his diary.

That night he said the band stayed in a Brooklyn loft by the Williamsburg Bridge, adding that "Jim goes into Manhattan tomorrow to find a drum pedal."

The next night was CBGB, another victory that Adams glossed over in favor of the trials of the road.

"After we load out, we park across Bowery," he wrote. "While John and Larissa are changing, some guy tries to break into the van. So we take a half hour driving the van to SoHo and work out shifts so that the van will be guarded."

That wasn't the whole story.

"Actually, we were shooting dope in the back of the van," Brannon says. "It was some fucking lowlife with a butter knife trying to break into our shit. You know, I pulled a needle out of my arm and I'm like, 'What the fuck, motherfucker,' you know, I picked up the tire iron and he's like, 'Whoa, whoa, whoa, whoa.' 'Cause we had a curtain and they didn't know we were in the back."

The drug use was a secret only if you didn't know what to look for. For Adams, as well as Kimball, when Brannon and Strickland would disappear, they were just spending some alone time.

Touring as a relatively unknown band, the Hyenas were still subject to a common malady of the day—cancelled shows. The layovers not only ate money but subjected the band to boredom, best quelled with intoxicants. Quarts of beer, joints of mid-level street weed, and whatever opiate could be found to keep the users in the band straight.

They met up at one point with Killdozer for some shows, who had along with them Davis, who would soon launch Creature Booking and become known as an obstreperous get-it-done agent with a formidable roster of talent.

The Hyenas enjoyed the band scene and the business end of it, entertained by the variety of personalities.

John and Larissa on stage at Bookies in Detroit in 1988.
Photo by Jon Howard.

But the best to hope for in terms of lodging was a relatively comfortable couch or floor as they killed time before the next gig, which sometimes could be over a week, as the small-band touring circuit was still getting established. Cancellations happened, and because of the paucity of venues, a band would look for a place to rehearse to stay sharp. A borrowed basement or another band's practice studio became a place to work out, as a band that was used to the rigor of everyday practice started to feel incomplete both musically and spiritually without that release.

"Larissa booked those tours, which could mean nine days of doing nothing," says Preston Long, who in the late eighties formed Wig in Ann Arbor, which became part of the Michigan scene as Long became friends with the Hyenas.

It seemed "like we were doing this touring as well as anyone can at that level," Monroe says.

On their first major road trip, Boston, Hoboken, and New York City had been triumphs. They'd been photographed by Monica Dee, a talented shooter whose record-sleeve credits included Pussy Galore, the Pandoras, and Phantom Tollbooth, for a piece in the fanzine *Away from the Pulsebeat.*

Lulls were a temporary setback, as the band, stationed in Brannon's van, made its way south from New York to Washington, DC. Opening for Fugazi, the Hyenas played to a full house at DC Space.

"From the moment they went on stage, it was clear to me that we were going on a journey," Fugazi singer Ian MacKaye wrote decades later in the liner notes for a reissue of Hyenas records.

The next day, an in-store in Philly was cancelled, but the Hyenas played a house party not far from the University of Pennsylvania campus. Thurston Moore and Steve Shelley from Sonic Youth made the trek to catch the show and left impressed. Sonic Youth at the time was working on songs that would be *Daydream Nation*, the album that would catapult them to the major-label big time.

Strickland, meanwhile, was working her social connecting magic, making friends with Moore, an influential tastemaker and enthusiastic backer of solid sounds.

"Larissa knew how to make friends; she was good at making social connections," Monroe says. She didn't use phony showbiz overtures; Strickland was a true fan and admirer of some musicians. It ended up helping the Hyenas move as far forward as they could.

The band blew off Pittsburgh and the Electric Banana, a small venue that hosted mostly local bands. Its reputation wasn't the best; some bands claimed they hadn't been paid their guarantees. The show was a last-minute add, anyway. Instead, they shelled out thirty-five bucks for a night at a Days Inn. After couch surfing for a week, it was a welcome respite.

"We rarely stayed in hotels," Monroe says. They were choosy about where they stayed, and at this point the Hyenas were mostly happy to be with each other, as if in a platoon infiltrating enemy territory.

"We would try to stay with people who didn't talk too much," he says.

The next night, April 2, at the University of Cincinnati, Adams wrote in his tour diary, "This couple had a baby with them. They actually had John kiss the baby while the band played! When John and Larissa asked the parents why they had brought their child to the show, the parents replied, 'She's seen all the Touch and Go bands.'"

Buffalo, New York; South Bend, Indiana; and Madison, Wisconsin, followed.

In South Bend, Rusk and then-wife Lisa, the team that ran Touch and Go, showed up, as well as Steve Albini with former Scratch Acid drummer Rey Washam.

"Corey and Lisa told the band to expect an LP recording session in August and there are real possibilities for Europe, both record-release-wise and for touring," Adams reported.

At O'Cayz Corral in Madison, Butch Vig mixed sound as the band again opened for Die Kreuzen.

From there, the band drove up to Minneapolis, where

they stayed with *Your Flesh*'s Davis.

"They were well on their way at that point," Davis says. After the show, the band came back to Davis's loft in a revamped downtown building and listened to music. Strickland talked for a while with Bill Hobson of the night's headliner, Killdozer.

The Hyenas were getting a professional appraisal of their work, and with their shows being checked out by influential people like Moore from Sonic Youth and Albini, they were drawing people from what would become a lucrative, popularly acclaimed indie rock industry.

The reviews of *Merry Go Round* came in solid.

"The guttural vomiting Brannon passes off as singing is more than just delightful, it's a heady fuse of bile leading to the walls of 'Stain.' The whole thing blows in a stinking cacophonic mess when, as he says, he comes 'down from above,'" Tucson bimonthly *Rhetoric Farm* wrote.

"While listening to this I kept imagining what it'd be like if Jim Morrison, in his drug-induced stupor, had cracked his skull trying to get on stage to do an impromptu set with Iggy and the Stooges," a reviewer for punk zine *Maximum Rocknroll* reported.

Boston's *Suburban Voice* focused on the vocals, noting Brannon's Negative Approach lineage. "He exhibits more soul; in fact it's the voice of a deeply tortured soul and a sound that's riveted with explosive tension . . ."

"Loud noisy annoying guitars, half sung/half screamed singing, pounding drums, loud base," said *Jersey Beat*, an East Coast fanzine.

Ink Disease, a Los Angeles punk zine, wrote, "This album

could almost be the soundtrack to an X-rated western."

Not everyone was smitten, as Minneapolis fanzine *Uncle Fester* said, "Maybe I was expecting too much from the Laughing Hyenas. Considering the hype they've gotten, what would you expect?"

Tour complete, the Hyenas loaded the gear back into the Platt Road house. Kimball went back to his job at Pizzeria Uno, and Monroe started taking Manpower temp jobs, hitchhiking to his assignments. He decided to quit the cab-driving gig.

Sticker from the Merry Go Round *era. Courtesy of Kevin Monroe.*

"It was good for writing stories, and it was certainly an influence as far as music writing," he says. "But was it a healthy lifestyle? Not at all."

Most of the Hyenas spent some time in the local jails, usually on minor charges of shoplifting, public drinking, or other low-level misdemeanors.

Monroe was having some legal problems stemming from

his absence from Ann Arbor; he'd been busted the year before for letting some kids drink in his cab, a misdemeanor.

He got a community service sentence, a common fallback for cops in college towns, where small-stuff offenses like Monroe's were disposed of easily.

But that meant he had to report to an officer of the court as part of the deal. And the live shows were taking up much of his time.

"The community service office was very lenient, and I took that to mean I could come and go as I pleased," Monroe says. "I got cavalier."

He failed to report for two monthly meetings in a row and received a court summons.

When he got there, he was taken into custody. He was an inmate at the Washtenaw County Jail. "It was right around the time I had a full Amish beard, this psychedelic leprechaun–looking thing," he says.

"You're going to do the rest of the time in jail," the judge said, meaning Monroe would be out of commission for six months. Recording and live dates would have to be postponed.

"But Larissa went to the court, had a meeting with the court officer and the judge; she went in there and pleaded her personal case," Monroe says.

She explained the band, the mounting success the group was having, the tour dates.

"He's a fuckup and we understand that and what's going on but putting him in jail would jeopardize all of our livelihoods," Strickland told the judge. She showed the booked tour dates later in the year, an easy task since the band was always booking shows. Strickland proposed he pay the fine and keep reporting.

The judge found it plausible. For all anyone knows, his kids could have been Hyenas fans. Monroe was fetched from his holding cell, where he'd been for a couple of days.

"I have no idea how it worked, but it did, and Larissa had gotten me out of jail," Monroe says.

The band were in a loose preproduction mode to put down their next record, basing the timing on what Rusk had told them at the South Bend show—recording with Vig again, at Smart Studios in Madison.

The band was so well rehearsed, most of the songs were ready to record, having been part of the show almost since Kimball joined a year before. A couple more, "New Gospel" and "Desolate Son," were composed, ready to go on what would be their debut LP.

The spare song they had recorded during the first session at Smart, "Candy," had been released on a four-song flexi-disc released with *The Bob* magazine that also featured Lime Spiders, the Bevis Frond, and Nikki Sudden. Flexis were a regular part of each issue, and the Hyenas landed a spot on one of the stronger discs.

Their momentum hit a roadblock.

Kimball's brother, Bruce, the Olympic champion, had faltered since winning the silver in 1984. He dropped out of the University of Michigan, where he had a diving scholarship. He drank heavily, started using coke, and took a pizza delivery job. He continued to train and hoped to make the Olympic trials in 1988.

Bruce Kimball went with his father to Tampa, Florida, in July, where the elder Kimball taught at a summer diving camp. Bruce would continue his training there, as the trials were to begin in later August.

On the evening of August 1, Bruce Kimball left his daily training and hit a local bar with a friend. Later that evening, he was heading to his friend's rural home outside Tampa, inadvertently sped past the driveway, and plowed through a group of thirty to forty teenagers, many underaged and drinking, gathered at a meeting place called "the Spot."

Two kids died, six were injured.

"It was this gap in my life," Jim Kimball says. "We were getting ready to record the album, and this happening with my brother—I was distracted."

The legal wrangling, the impact of the crime, and the public outrage over the tragedy was felt deeply around the house on Platt.

"I got to say that it took a toll on the band emotionally," Brannon adds. "It was very hard on Jim. His brother was like his hero. We had to step back, of course, and give him time. And of course, at the time were like, still, the Monkees, living together, touring together, being together."

After a month down, the band in September headed out for shows in Columbia, Missouri, and Lawrence, Kansas, before heading north to Madison to record its first full-length album. The title was not yet decided, but the band continued to read from the Southern Gothic genre, an enduring influence.

SIDE 4

Some of the songs for *Can't Pray a Lie*, the name of the new LP, were over a year old. By the time they pulled into Madison and Smart Studios in the fall of 1988, the Laughing Hyenas were ready to get the songs down and move on.

"I had never seen a band record, but it was clear the Hyenas had this very smooth working relationship with Butch [Vig]," says Bruce Adams, who drove the band to Wisconsin for the recording sessions. Again, Touch and Go owner Corey Rusk insisted they use Vig at the control board. The numbers were right—$1,780 to record, another $180 for the hotel—and the band was familiar with the place.

"Butch knew what they wanted, and he would make measured suggestions, mostly about overdubs," says Adams, who assumed the role of gofer, offering no opinions, grabbing Brannon some beer when he needed it to avoid breaking the flow of recording. "They were super focused; it was really interesting to see them do this."

As roadie for the first tour, Adams had become accustomed to the inevitable push-and-pull of placing four different personalities in a van and shipping them around the country.

Vig handled the four Hyenas easily, although the volume and the sounds were still new and unique to him, even though it had only been a year since *Merry Go Round*.

"Here was this guy whose own bands were nothing like the Hyenas," Adams says. "But he had a real respect for what they were trying to do."

Vig was at the time the drummer for Fire Town, a college-radio-friendly pop band with debts to R.E.M. and the Beatles. But he understood the Hyenas and really appreciated how they showed up on the studio doorstep fully rehearsed and ready to roll.

"The songs were in good shape," Vig says. "There was no time for preproduction or time to build the songs. They came in and ran through the songs."

Then the tape ran.

The band eschewed overdubs, but "there were a few," Vig says. "Every now and then I could get Larissa to double-track the guitar. It was minimal. And there were a few extra tracks done on vocals, and sometimes I could get John to go back and sing those if I wanted more options. I would say 80 percent of the songs were live takes."

It was an easier record to lay down, Kimball says, as the songs had been in the set list for almost a year.

"We had it figured out," he says. "We spent so many hours in the basement for that record, once we got in there everything was right on. We got more low end, and Butch Vig was evolving."

Another five days, another record, with eight freshly recorded songs.

The name of the album was cribbed from a chapter in Mark Twain's 1885 book *Huckleberry Finn*. The Southern

Gothic influence remained in full effect, as Strickland's love of literature shone through. The cover art—an angelic-looking young woman, looking up as if to heaven—came from an aged book on angels that Strickland owned. The design was done by Dave and Christine Linabury, local artists and friends of Strickland.

The back cover featured cherubic faces amid beds of flowers and vines, done in a brown tint as color was too expensive for the Touch and Go budget.

The song-title lettering was a purple scribble done by a young child from a local preschool. The design was pure art, a package that was more than music.

"Larissa was in charge of that 100 percent," Kimball says.

Brannon, though, had some input: "The matrix on *You Can't Pray a Lie* on one side is 'We'll come into your town,' and the other side is 'We'll help you party it down,'" he says proudly, lifting the iconic lyric from the Grand Funk Railroad hit of 1974, "We're an American Band."

It could have been well adapted to the Hyenas traveling road show, which was heading back to Ann Arbor to pick up some boxes of T-shirts before again leaving to play some dates with Sonic Youth.

Sonic Youth wrapped recording *Daydream Nation*, a double LP, in August 1988, and the album was slated for an October 18 release. The band had just returned from ten dates in Europe and were much like the Hyenas in that each of the four members was advanced, accomplished, and diligent in their craft.

Sonic Youth drummer Steve Shelley was raised in Midland, Michigan, and was an enthusiastic and supportive fan of Strickland during her time in L-Seven, while Thurston Moore was an admirer of Negative Approach, the Hyenas, and Brannon.

Larissa with Thurston Moore and Steve Shelley from Sonic Youth backstage at Liberty Lunch in Austin, Texas. Courtesy of Kevin Monroe.

They'd already made the drive to see the Hyenas play a house party in Philadelphia earlier in the year and were sold. They asked the Hyenas to support them for a series of shows, with Sonic Youth headlining, Die Kreuzen in the middle for some of the dates, and the Hyenas opening.

This time, the touring finance mechanism was set. Each Hyena got five dollars a day to live. There would usually be a meal provided at the venue, so the money had to cover breakfast and lunch, as well as cigarettes and beer, if the gig didn't provide it.

Strickland lived on apples and Marlboros, while Kimball saved his money from his pizzeria job so he wouldn't be scrounging. Monroe was a nimble shoplifter, which extended his per diem. Brannon, while savvy in most ways, was feckless when it came to basic survival.

"We'd be in New York and breakfast was $2.99, which was too much for John and Larissa," Kimball says. One night in New York, Kimball and Brannon headed out to get a slice of pizza, and while they were walking down the street they looked in the window of a higher-end Italian place.

"Oh my God, look, that's Roland Gift," Brannon said, peering both at the singer of the Fine Young Cannibals and the chicken tetrazzini on his plate.

"It was unreal how John could spot things like that," Kimball says. "We're hungry. Who notices that?"

The connection with Sonic Youth was also helped by Strickland's ability to talk shop—touring, recording, marketing—with the band. She was engaged in art and business, and did a good job, most of the time, with both.

"One of our first gigs was with Sonic Youth, in Detroit," Brannon says. "We were already friends. So when they asked, 'Do you want to tour?,' we were like, kind of, the new, young hip band. That's when we cut our teeth touring. I'd never been exposed to that kind of touring. Before, we'd been doing live things but always sporadic shit. [Sonic Youth] were just coming up, everyone knew who they were, but the venues were bigger."

They started at the Ritz in New York, with a 2,500 capacity, a Friday night show that included Die Kreuzen.

"I had never heard of Sonic Youth before we played with them," Kimball says.

The tour moved upstate to Syracuse, then down to Columbus and Cleveland, Ohio; Toronto, Ontario; Detroit, Chicago, Madison, and wrapping in Minneapolis. Almost every venue held at least a thousand people, and most of the shows were sold out.

"At that point, for us as a new band just starting out, for

them to take us under their wing, because at that point we were like, 'Fuck, we got this record out and nobody knows who the fuck we are,' they really exposed us to the whole indie rock college circuit," Brannon says.

The money was fair, with advance ticket prices running between $8 and $13. The Hyenas got between $300 and $500 a night—the most they would make during their existence. They added merchandise money, selling T-shirts for $12 a pop along with copies of *Merry Go Round*.

"They were paying us," says Brannon. "I don't remember slumming."

Sonic Youth was also willing to overlook the band's habits, which Monroe was not immune to.

"We all went out to dinner one night and me and Kevin passed out in our plates of food," Brannon says. "Then we came to, and Kim Gordon was just sitting there, eating with a smile on her face like nothing happened. They knew we were fucked up. They were just, like, going on like nothing was nothing. They were very nice to us. You know, it couldn't have been that bad 'cause they asked us later to do part of the *Goo* tour too."

Their relatively good life on the road was a different story once they got back to Ann Arbor and the Platt house. The Hyenas went from playing for up to a thousand people to scratching out a living among folks who just thought they were weird.

Their day jobs were spotty, although being in a college town made it easier to get fleeting, temporary work. Monroe kept busy through Manpower and got a job as a cashier selling textbooks at a campus bookstore. Kimball hung in at the pizza place. Strickland and Brannon went back to their jobs, making minimum wage.

Kimball still didn't know of the drug habits. He stayed to himself on Platt, even keeping his food in his room. A loner by nature, Kimball took long walks with his dog and kept close with his family, especially in the wake of his brother's legal problems.

"I lived with this guy for like three or four years," Brannon says. "I never remember one point where I had a beer with him sitting at the couch. But he is a great musician."

For Brannon and Strickland, keeping themselves medicated helped them maintain their creativity, for the time being. They fed into the ideas of the more prolific Monroe.

"I'd always been in bands where I wrote a lot of the music," Brannon says. But he started hearing the rest of them come up with songs that were better than his.

"They just had all these ideas, these really great ideas," he says. "So I just concentrated on the lyrics and the singing. I threw some music in there, but Larissa and Kevin were writing some really good things, and Kevin was coming up with great bass lines."

Songwriter publishing was never a consideration, although it's the crux of so much litigation down the road, usually once a left-out band member learns of the financial possibilities.

For the Hyenas, there were no individual songwriting credits.

"It's not who writes it, it's the people playing it," Brannon says. "At the end of the day, one person maybe comes up with the riff or the beat, but everyone throws down to make the song. With the Hyenas, it [was] a layering thing. So we'd never do a 'written by' thing."

The new LP was being pressed, but the band was busy

in the basement, their laboratory, cooking up new material.

Hyenas sets were getting longer to accommodate the new material, and they were starting to headline more shows, slowly growing a regional base. Shows in Detroit, Lansing, Kalamazoo, and Ann Arbor were becoming events, social occasions with a dramatic, powerful musical backdrop.

The year 1988 faded into winter, cold and dark.

In January 1989 Kimball flew to Florida with his family to attend the trial of his brother, Bruce, charged with DUI manslaughter and DUI causing serious bodily injury.

Their stay was brief as Bruce Kimball pleaded guilty, thus avoiding the trial.

"I cannot put the families of these kids through it," he told one of his lawyers.

At his sentencing three weeks later, Kimball changed his plea to "no contest."

He got seventeen years in prison, followed by fifteen years of probation.

In late February 1989, a month before *You Can't Pray a Lie* came out, the band played at the Eastern Michigan University campus in Ypsilanti, Michigan, ten minutes from the Platt house.

The flyer, designed by Monroe, featured more ornate, decayed drawings, with a Bible verse at the bottom: "Be not forgetful to entertain strangers: for thereby some have entertained angels unaware. —Heb. 13:2."

"I once hitchhiked and got a ride with a truck driver who was a bit of a Bible thumper," Monroe says. After twenty-five minutes of the driver witnessing, they arrived at Monroe's destination. "I put that Bible verse on his steamed windows with my finger and said goodbye, and I could see him looking it up quickly as I jumped over the median and disappeared."

While their music was frequently received as an angry outburst from a quartet led by junkies, which it was, they also carried the souls of biblical poets.

It was complicated and about to get even more tangled.

SIDE 5

J on Spencer, guitarist and vocalist for Pussy Galore, wrote Brannon a letter in early spring 1989: "Dear John— thanks for the record, it's great. I especially like 'Love's My Only Crime,' 'Sister,' and the last song on side 1 ('Lullaby'?)."

He noted that his band was touring in the summer, and he put in a word with his booker to get the Hyenas on some of their bills.

"Say hello to Larissa + all the other Hyenas," he signed off.

You Can't Pray a Lie came out in March, and the Hyenas prepared for another slew of dates. Touch and Go pressed 3,000 vinyl copies with 1,259 cassettes.

A month after the LP came out, the Hyenas paused for another tragedy that affected everyone.

Monroe's sister, Brittain, died at eighteen of leukemia in April 1989. She was a twin, one of three of Monroe's siblings.

As Brittain's conditioned had worsened, the band for the first and only time cancelled a show, scheduled in Washington, DC.

Instead, the band insisted Monroe fly to Minnesota,

where his sister was being treated, tapping the band fund to pay for it.

"It was during the darkest days of my drug use," Monroe says. "I went to Minnesota where she died; she was at a clinic there for treatment. It was a rough time for everyone."

Again, Brannon took it as hard as anyone, having a bit of phobia about death anyway.

"We were definitely all feeling the shit," he says. "It really was just a bad time for everyone."

It took some time to regroup. They stuck around the Midwest for the first part of the year, doing occasional treks to Canada and the East Coast, as their legend both at home and away continued to build.

Motorbooty magazine, cofounded by Big Chief guitarist and lauded artist Mark Dancey, called the Laughing Hyenas "glory bound bastards" in its second issue, praise that was echoed throughout the undercurrent of the music scene both locally and nationally. As *You Can't Pray* a Lie hit the stores, *Merry Go Round* became more widely available, and the live show kept getting stronger.

Reviews of the new LP were strong and were starting to focus on Brannon and that voice.

Ink Disease wrote, "Your better vocalists won't just 'sing,' but will use their voices as instruments. . . . Hyena John Brannon does it to show us an unheard-of sense of total desperation. That's what this band sounds like. Desperation . . . It's loud, it's painful and when you hear it, you certainly can't ignore it. Perhaps the fact that you can't ignore it is the greatest compliment you can give a band."

Maximum Rockandroll said *Pray* was "musical exorcism . . . five stars, 100% A+, an essential release."

The record was also scoring some college-radio play,

ranking fifth on a list curated by *College Media Journal*, a slick publication for college radio programmers.

Record stores in Minneapolis and Los Angeles reported high sales while the record landed on *CMJ*'s Top 100 list at #51 in May. College stations on the East Coast put the Hyenas among their top played records, and Northwestern University's WNUR, an influential Midwest station, named it a top-requested LP.

"Love's My Only Crime" was named an "emphasis" track, making it a possible single.

At WRFL, the University of Kentucky's student station, the Hyenas were feted not only as a frequent play but also played the station's music festival.

"The Hyenas roared out (if you've seen 'em, you'd prob'ly agree with the chosen verb) to an extra enthusiastic house with lead throat John Brannon retaining his title as angriest front man alive," wrote WRFL Program Director Mick Jeffries.

Montreal bimonthly *RearGarde* put Strickland on its cover and published an interview with Brannon inside.

"The Laughing Hyenas are hot—and they know it," read the interview intro. "The Ann Arbor foursome rolled into town [in May 1989] on the heels of a brand-new album, *You Can't Pray a Lie*, and put on one hell of a show at Foufounes. . . . The band's successful hybrid of hard rock, psychedelic blues fusion has dealt them a good hand, and live, well live, they are awesome—an incredible fury of untamed sound."

Asked about how the records were evolving, Brannon promised, "They'll get better as we progress. I don't think we've captured our live sound yet. We really want to project onto vinyl what we do live. We want to capture that rawness. Playing live is really what we're all about."

The interviewer asked about remaining in Ann Arbor.

"We travel around quite a bit, so it's not like we get sick of where we're living," Brannon said. "It's a good place to base ourselves because we have a house, and we can practice there. Generally, though, we keep a low profile."

The interviews became an opportunity to spread their gospel. They enjoyed the interactions, particularly Brannon, who was a forceful, charismatic subject.

It was never a threat to Monroe or Kimball, who rarely said anything if they were asked to be part of the conversation. "It was John and Larissa's band," Kimball says.

Plus, while they were making fans, it still wasn't profitable.

"We were not living very well on the *Can't Pray a Lie* tour," Kimball says.

At a show in Connecticut, they were slotted into a bill with "five straight-edge punk bands," Kimball says. It was held in a large hall that featured several events at a time, including weddings.

Kimball began wandering around and came upon a large ballroom where a wedding reception was being held.

"I looked normal and walked into this room and put all this food on a plate and walked out," he says. "No one said a thing."

He came back to the gig, where Brannon, Strickland, and Monroe were standing by the merchandise booth. They eyed the food, and Kimball told them where to find it.

"They all went down there and got kicked out," Kimball says. "They didn't fit in."

The band moved down the East Coast for a sold-out show in June at the Ritz in New York, opening for Mudhoney and Sonic Youth. The show was an occasion to honor Sonic Youth's signing to Geffen Records, a lucrative deal that was the start of corporate acceptance of alternative music.

In the audience were members of Nirvana, who, like the Hyenas, were still shoestring touring.

It was clear to the industry that there was money to be made, and labels were scouting for bands that could navigate the gulf between street cred and sales.

Bands that had launched with no intention or hope of ever making mass-marketed music were targeted by the suits, who cloaked themselves in the same garb worn by the bands, many of whom could afford nothing better.

While the commercial airwaves were dominated by Guns N' Roses, Mötley Crüe, and Poison, bean counters were seeing dollar signs in the alternative movement. Hüsker Dü, Jane's Addiction, and Soundgarden all had signed major-label deals.

Sonic Youth were perfect for joining that mainstream drift, a professional operation with camera-ready looks and music that was edgy, even deep, but not provocative enough to alienate consumers. People could go see Sonic Youth after work and go back in the next morning and talk about it, as if it were a movie or a play. They were neither confrontational nor intimidating. They didn't leave a mark but were intensely creative and original.

"'Alternative' never interested us," drummer Steve Shelley told *Your Flesh* mag in 1999. "It was a sales format for radio stations who'd given up on soft metal. . . . We're more organic than that. . . . I feel we are truly an independent band."

The Hyenas delivered another dynamic show in New York, but the crowd that went to see the newly signed Sonic Youth was different from before.

"The Ritz crowd, which was described by some as being 'Nitzer Ebbish,' were baffled by the Laughing Hyenas," wrote Greg Baise for *Michigan Daily*, who was in New York covering the New Music Seminar, a music festival similar to early South by Southwest conferences. "Most of them just stood there in terror, as John Brannon's incomprehensible vocals ruptured many an eardrum, and John Brannon's spit removed much white makeup from the faces of the boys and girls in the crowd."

Baise's account echoes what others had seen when confronted by the Hyenas.

"The band started, and as soon as John started singing, you could actually see the people in front take a step back," says Bruce Adams, the former roadie who was now working in marketing for Touch and Go.

After the Ritz show, Brannon and Kurt Cobain from Nirvana met backstage. The two talked a bit about recording, venues, and touring, as both bands were at a mid-level of industry buzz, still toiling on van tours.

John and Kevin in the van. Courtesy of Kevin Monroe.

Brannon praised the work of Butch Vig at Smart Studios. Cobain had heard *Pray* and was also a fan of the Killdozer recordings.

"We really dig the sound of your records," Cobain told Brannon.

"Well, go to Butch Vig," Brannon said.

"Sure enough, they got up on that," Brannon says years later. "And it was the perfect mix for that whole deal."

The Hyenas played in New Brunswick, New Jersey, on the same trip, and Monroe, Kimball, and Brannon gave an interview to *Dagger*, a New Jersey fanzine, conducted by Ken Salerno, a respected chronicler of the local music scene.

It was the most complete Hyenas interview to date, a four-page spread that touched on songwriting, the early frustration with finding a label, Kimball's joining the band, and recording with Butch Vig, who was still unknown at the time.

Asked about the thirty-minute length of *Pray*, Brannon said, "I don't think it's too good to put like a million songs on an album," unknowingly—but wisely—presaging the CD era, in which listeners were blitzed with a wrong-headed notion that more is better.

"You get real burned out with too many songs."

They spoke glowingly of Touch and Go—"No contracts . . . just a handshake," Monroe said—and their overseas distribution, which consisted of outlets in Germany, Holland, and England.

"Have you guys gone to Europe yet?" Salerno asked.

It was already in the works, Kimball said.

Touring the US in the second half of the year became

difficult for the Hyenas, as they again endured long slack periods on the road. They weren't big enough to headline anything more than a small club, and so they were reliant on connecting with bigger draws to stay afloat. They needed that boost to get to the next level.

Strickland called Peter Davis, the *Your Flesh* publisher. He had formed Creature Booking and had an impressive roster that included most of the groups on the Amphetamine Reptile label, including God Bullies, Cows, and Surgery.

Flier for a local show. Courtesy of Kevin Monroe.

"The Hyenas were getting this great street reverence," says Davis, who began to book them on some Midwest sorties. "And they were starting to draw. The money was okay, between $250 and $500 guarantees, depending on the market. It wasn't barnstormers, though, and it should have been."

Davis knew that heroin was a part of their scene—"It wasn't even the five-hundred pound gorilla in the room, it was right there"—but the band never stiffed him on money, always showed up at shows on time and delivered.

"They never called and asked me for money," Davis says. "I put trust in the bands to follow through on obligations. I felt like they were on their way, but I feared they could become their worst enemies."

After some Davis-booked dates in mid-1989, they wanted more. But some of the promoters he dealt with were quietly voicing reservations about the drugs.

"I have to pass," Davis told Strickland. "I'm just getting some pushback."

The fall was initially slated to be a West Coast swing, and booking it on their own wasn't working out.

Instead, an opportunity arose to tour Europe with labelmates Killdozer. They'd been there twice already and had a following.

To get to Europe, Corey Rusk at Touch and Go asked each member to kick in $300 for airfare and he would get the rest.

"I gave Larissa $300 to go to the bank for the cashier's check to send Corey," Kimball says. "Two weeks later, she came back and said I only gave her $100. I told her I gave her $300 and if she didn't figure this out, I was quitting."

On the eve of a European tour, it would have left the Hyenas out of the picture.

"So she all of a sudden found the money," Kimball says.

●

The flight from New York to Amsterdam took seven hours, time spent with the last of the drugs wearing off and sitting in coach. Thankfully, they could still smoke on international flights.

Once on the ground, they'd have to clear customs, meet their tour manager with the vehicle, and travel into the city. It would be dicey for Brannon and Strickland. Their habits needed tending, and while they had enough to get them into the air, by the time they got everything together on the ground in Amsterdam, they would need to score.

"When we first landed in Amsterdam, I told Larissa, 'Listen, if you need to get something, please do not do it on your own,'" Monroe says. "'Just let me do it, okay?' I begged her. 'Do not do anything by yourself.'"

Things initially went smoothly, and their retinue—three Killdozers, four Hyenas, and a tour manager—went to the hotel. It was early in the day, and too early to check in, so the luggage and guitars were left behind the front desk.

"There's a coffeehouse just a block away," the desk clerk, also one of the owners, told the road manager.

They all gathered at the foot of a stairway leading to the street, down six steps.

Before they could get out the front door, Strickland told them to wait. "I'll be right back," she said.

Strickland approached the clerk who had graciously directed them to the coffee shop.

She was sick and desperate.

"Where can I score?" she asked.

The others stood waiting when "one guitar and then another came down the steps," says Killdozer vocalist-bassist Michael Gerald. It was followed by the owner screaming, "Get out!" They'd stayed at the hotel before on previous visits, so this episode was a little personal.

"We had no idea [the Hyenas] had this heroin problem," Gerald says. "We'd been asked if we minded sharing a van with them on this tour. But no one told me why we might mind."

That was the starting point for a rough tour.

"I'm not sure what made her think that Amsterdam was cool about heroin," he says.

The tour proceeded and the Hyenas delivered with the same intensity as they did stateside. Their records were well distributed, and people knew who they were. The itinerary took them through Holland, Germany, Austria, Switzerland, and the UK. Venues included Blixa Bargeld's club in Berlin and an open field festival, their first.

The rented gear didn't include drums, so the American bands had to make do with borrowing the sets of the opening local bands.

"Every show we played on a different drum kit," Kimball says. "These drum kits were from some yokel who never changed drumheads. So I would break the heads. One show, I broke both the top and the bottom heads of the snare."

Cymbals also fell prey to his punishing attack. It got so every night there was an equipment issue.

"Killdozer and the Hyenas alternated headlining each of the twenty-one stops, so on the nights the Hyenas opened, [Killdozer drummer] Dan Hobson had to play with a fucked-up snare," Kimball says.

The trip was dogged by the drug problem. Logistics were a fiasco.

"We had constant problems with Larissa," Gerald says. "Among the issues was finding her."

Yet the tour was a success in that both bands got plenty

of attention and performed well.

The Hyenas did a six-page interview with *No Trend Press*, a German-language fanzine in which they discussed the death penalty, violence, racism, cops, and music.

They mostly passed on the questions outside of music, which were college-freshman level in terms of intellect.

Brannon said he comes from a place, Detroit, where violence is part of the culture, "but that doesn't mean you have to be violent in order to survive. The whole culture, environment, music, and lyrics are influenced by it. We come from a very violent city, and I think it has influenced us."

Brannon mentioned Ron Asheton had said he'd be interested in producing the next Hyenas record, "but I don't know what his production skills are like. Besides, he was pretty [drunk] when he said that."

The band talked about their meager finances and dedicating most of their lives to the band.

"We don't have any money for things like food," Monroe said. "I'm three months behind on my rent, and I owe $1,600. We all have debts."

"You can't make money like that," the interviewer said.

Monroe noted that Fugazi were currently #7 on the German independent record charts.

"I know how Fugazi live," he said. "They live very cheaply. They have a house where they all sleep; they buy cheap food. They don't have eight video recorders, stereo systems, or great furniture. The money they make is just enough to cover costs for the records they put out and to keep making them."

At the end of the conversation, the interviewer asked, "Do you take drugs?"

Monroe fired back, "Us? No."

"What, no drugs at all?"

Brannon copped to it.

"Yes, but that has nothing to do with our music. It's not something we want to talk about or advocate."

When they returned to the US, "[Killdozer] wasn't happy about the whole trip, and Corey learned of it," Monroe says. Rusk called the house and asked some questions. He was running a flourishing label with bands that needed to get along, and a stunt like Strickland's jeopardized the situation.

"Corey knew it was a gamble, with Larissa and John, to send them to Europe," Adams says. "He knew they had drug problems, and they swore it was under control. But sometimes your friends let you down."

"Maybe we weren't the perfect touring partner for [Killdozer]," Monroe says. "You know, different people, different backgrounds."

It was resolved, and each party returned to their corner. But the Hyenas would not appear on another bill with Killdozer again.

Band money in the hands of Strickland was starting to become an issue. The plane fare to Europe was a symptom of a larger malady. Plus, she and Brannon were not getting along.

The band returned to play a homecoming gig at the Heidelberg in Ann Arbor, a German restaurant with an upstairs venue that had recently started hosting both national and local bands. Toward the end of their fifty-minute set, Brannon and Strickland publicly fought, the first time locals had seen the friction that the band was seeing more and more up close, both at home and on the road.

Strickland put down her guitar before the closing number and started to walk off the stage to her left, a slight flight of stairs in the compact, two-hundred-capacity venue. Brannon headed over—"What are you doing?"—as she stepped down, pushing away his hand as he tried to stop her and get a response. Kimball stood by impassively as Monroe fiddled with annoying solo bass runs, side-eyeing the exchange.

When Strickland reconsidered, she strapped on her guitar and let loose a hail of feedback—not the good kind—and Brannon told the crowd, "This is the last time you're gonna see my ass ever," before the band rolled into a new, unnamed song that never made the grade for release.

Brannon and Strickland were starting to fight as much as play. The rancor ranged from petty arguments about workload, with Strickland always feeling besieged by band business, to onstage disputes.

The acrimony was hard on Brannon, as Strickland was his first love. Now, amid festering heroin habits and a band that needed all the energy it would muster to break through, the sailing was getting rough.

They weren't out of the game; by the end of 1989, they began working on new songs.

But in Ann Arbor, no one now worked a day job except Kimball.

"For *Merry Go Round*, it seemed they were a happy couple," Kimball says. "Then at this point, they were not happy together. John would get really angry, 'Tune your fucking guitar,' right onstage."

The tension was enough for the drummer to move out at the end of 1989 and into his parents' house.

SIDE 6

The Laughing Hyenas are like fuckin' action figures, Jim Magas thought when he arrived in Ann Arbor in early 1990.

The band had become a legend, very quickly, and a furtive sighting of a member was something people talked about.

Magas had moved around, from his native Upper Michigan to a failed start at Central Michigan University, to Fort Worth, Texas, and back to the Midwest, finally landing in Ann Arbor.

He was a musician and eager to find out what the town had to offer. He was taken with the place immediately. The stories alone enthralled him.

Tales ranged from Brannon walking around in a trench coat with his shoulder-length black tresses, heading into record stores with blank cassettes and asking awed store workers to record the latest blues record for him, to Monroe's besuited, fabled street preaching.

Monroe remained a curious spectacle, hitchhiking around the small college town in a top hat. You'd hear rumors he was at the campus, on the Quad, the outdoor cultural center of the University of Michigan, barefoot and spouting scripture.

A Strickland sighting was rarest, always striking in a classy vintage dress, and despite her modest, provincial hairstyle and approachable demeanor, she always looked like the queen of the scene.

"GG Allin and Dee Dee Ramone were also both living in Ann Arbor around that time, so you had all this music," Magas says.

But the big game in town was the Hyenas, and meeting a Hyena was just as good, if not better, than a Ramone, a suicidal scuzz-rocker, or even a declining Stooge or MC5-er.

"What's the deal!?" Brannon shouted into Magas's face when they first met at the Blind Pig. It was a standard Brannon greeting, not meant in hostility but as a convivial conversation starter. A friendship began.

By spring 1990, the Platt house was no longer Hyenas headquarters. They lived . . . wherever they could. Strickland and Brannon got an apartment off Packard Street, not far from a basement apartment Magas rented on the same street, a main artery of the town.

Hanging out with Brannon, and sometimes Strickland, was a taxing but rewarding experience, Magas found. They'd get 40-ouncers of Budweiser, slap on some music, or—better as far as Brannon was concerned—*Yo! MTV Raps*, a show on MTV featuring rap videos, commentary, and interviews.

"We would be trying to go somewhere, and Brannon would be watching and it would be, 'Wait, one more video before we go,'" Magas says.

The Hyenas now rehearsed after hours at Robey Tires, a storefront not far from downtown, where Monroe also slept at times. There was a lot of friction in the band, felt most acutely by Kimball, who was only in it for the music and had no patience for band drama.

There was so little money, rent for Brannon or Strickland was a target date to come up with any kind of payment possible. Gigs helped, and now that they could no longer count on Kimball bringing home leftover pizza, Brannon perfected his dumpster-dining/diving routine. Restaurants routinely dump leftover, prepared food at the end of the day. McDonald's could be a five-star dining experience for someone starving, as employees closing the store would toss Filet-O-Fish, Big Macs, apple pies—all packaged and untouched—into the trash bin.

Even when he had money, Brannon would suggest checking the garbage behind a restaurant to his colleagues.

The band was starting to write a new batch of songs, with heavier input from Brannon this time around, even working through some guitar parts with Strickland.

Again, there were to be no individual songwriting credits; this was a band.

In 1990, the Hyenas began a new practice of quarterly Saturday night shows at the Heidelberg, which had grown as a venue as it brought in some Touch and Go and Amphetamine Reptile bands.

The Hyenas shows became social occasions with live music. Brannon also began drawing a local coterie of short-skirted female admirers, small-town but groupies nonetheless, and they were sometimes a sanctuary for his self-inflicted financial woes. They didn't mind buying beer for the local hero.

"There was this sea of younger people getting into [the shows]," says Bruce Adams, who in 1990 was working in promotion for Touch and Go.

Their out-of-town forays continued, weekends on the

East Coast, interminable drives passed in silence save for the eternal tape deck.

Anyone but Kimball drove, Strickland most insistently and yet the most feared driver aside from the drummer.

They'd be done for the evening, say a Monday night show at Club Soda in Kalamazoo, and Strickland would insist she was ready to drive the hundred miles back at 3:00 a.m.

"She'd sit in the passenger seat and tell us she was ready to drive and then doze off with a cigarette in her hand, which then fell down and touched her leg," Kimball says. It sat burning the skin of her bare leg for fifteen seconds, Strickland basically unconscious, before she came to, hit the cigarette, and again announced she was ready to drive.

Monroe drove the most, as he was the heartiest. He kept a wooden box of cassettes, a smattering of Grateful Dead and a few other selections that didn't go over well. But if there was a nighttime drive, while everyone dozed, Monroe slapped on an unbearable version of "Dark Star" and enjoyed the highway trance. Occasionally, someone would "lose" a particularly annoying Dead cassette, or would awaken, pull it out of the deck, and toss it out the window.

"Larissa was driving one night, and she thought everyone was asleep, but I wasn't," Kimball says. She kept a brief cassette with four songs, her favorites on it. It included "Silver Rocket" by Sonic Youth and "Family Affair" by Sly and the Family Stone.

"She played it over and over when she thought everyone was sleeping," Kimball says.

Something in that predictable repetition appealed to her. It was something she could control.

●

In April 1990, Nirvana was playing in Madison, Wisconsin, at Club Underground. The next day, the band spent five days at Smart Studios, where they recorded several songs with Butch Vig, including a version of "Polly," a song that would end up on their iconic *Nevermind* album.

Nirvana's visit to Smart has several stories behind it. One is that Cobain's talk with Brannon in New York the previous year put Vig on his radar. The other is that Sub Pop chief Jonathan Poneman loved the sound of Killdozer's *Twelve-Point Buck* LP, recorded at Smart, and wanted to capture something similar for Nirvana's second full-length.

A few days after recording at Smart, Nirvana came to Ann Arbor, still unheralded for the most part as the opening band for the Flaming Lips.

They stayed at the new apartment Brannon and Strickland were renting. The first thing Brannon noticed was that Cobain was hurting. Six years Brannon's junior, he'd been doing heroin off and on since he was twenty.

They had more than dope in common. Both lived for music, from the dark blues of Son House to the pugnacious blare of the Stooges.

But while Brannon was a social, sometimes charming creature, Cobain was withdrawn and remote. They couldn't connect.

"Kurt crashed on my floor, and he was all sick," Brannon says. The cause was a failure to score, yet "we weren't putting it together. But we had shitloads of heroin on us. We could have gotten him straight."

Instead, Cobain pulled out some of Brannon's blues records and slapped on a Lead Belly platter, entranced by a song called "In the Pines."

●

Once Corey Rusk at Touch and Go started working with a band, he assumed the relationship would continue. With Rusk and the band having an established relationship and two releases under their belt, he no longer approached the Hyenas with recording dates; he figured that when they had the songs, they would let him know.

It was a marked difference than most labels, major and indie, in that they were often quicker to cut ties with an underperforming act. Rusk determined recording budgets in accordance with how the previous records performed.

John Brannon and Butch Vig at Smart Studios recording Life of Crime. *Courtesy of John Brannon.*

By the time the band started what would become *Life of Crime* at Smart Studios in June 1990, the previous records had sold modestly. Still, the live shows drew consistently and the Hyenas received solid reviews. The budget for *Life of Crime* was $2,830, with another $240 on nights at the Red Roof Inn in Madison.

The songs were the strongest yet, but Kimball was distressed by the escalated feuding between Brannon and Strickland—"All the time, yelling at each other," he says. "And Larissa was diminishing; she was really struggling."

The record was sonically improved by Monroe's new equipment purchases, and the stronger rig drove a bigger, thicker bass sound.

"I had a new bass, a Fender Jazz, and I played through a Kustom cabinet that my dad had used back in his band days," Monroe says. The cabinet had two fifteen-inch speakers that he modified to handle four hundred watts each.

Vig, too, was getting better every time he recorded someone. The studio went from eight to sixteen tracks in 1987 and to twenty-four tracks in 1990.

This session was the first time Vig noticed some strains in the band.

"I could sense the tension," he says. "There was not a lot, but I could sense more."

At the same time, "they had gotten more sophisticated in writing arrangements," Vig says. "It was a natural evolution, but they still based everything on the live performance. What we did in the studio approximated what they did onstage."

Strickland was growing as a musician beyond what Brannon ever envisioned.

"She became a real stylized guitar player," Brannon says.

"That was the beauty of it. You start from nothing, you have an idea of where you want to lean, and then you come up with your own shit along the way. Starting from scratch is the best way."

The recording was delayed by an actual life of crime, albeit very petty. One afternoon, during the final mix, the band was to meet Vig at the studio around midday.

Shortly before the band left the hotel, Brannon and Strickland headed to the grocery store, Brannon with money in his pocket. It wasn't a ruse to score or get high; they were really going to the store.

When they didn't arrive at the studio at the appointed time, Vig thought "they must have gotten arrested."

They'd always been punctual. Four hours later, still no band. It was five hours before they showed up, sheepish.

Brannon had been arrested stealing—wait for it—string cheese in Wisconsin, a state known worldwide as the "cheese state" for its prolific output.

"We had to stay in Madison an extra day," Kimball says. "He went to court and the judge made him write a five-hundred-word essay on why you shouldn't steal cheese in Wisconsin."

The cover art for *Life of Crime* was done by Bill Widener, a revered graphic and comic book artist from Kentucky. His *Go-Man!* cyberpunk comic series was a hit among fans of underground comics, and he was also a friend of Brannon's.

The budget called for only black-and-white for the *Life of Crime* cover, so Widener delivered a fine, simple graphic featuring a black heart with four arrows stuck into it, with tattered lettering. The back was more Widener lettering augmented by Monroe's and Strickland's own devilish touches that included allusions to rogue angels, whiskey, pool halls, and card games.

The songs included a straight but brutal cover of "Life of Crime" by the Weirdos.

From Madison, the band kept moving, through the Midwest and back to the East Coast, where they almost lost Kimball.

The band had been traveling, earning their money here and there, and Monroe, Brannon, and Strickland were deep in their habits. Heroin was easy to get, but the only money they had came from the gigs, and that was band money. The temptation to loot the kitty was too great, the need for drugs too overpowering for any one of them to hang on to the money. Kimball was the man holding the cash.

By the time they hit New York, the band had rolled up $1,400 in band funds. He went out to buy some food for himself, and reflexively pulled out his wallet, flashing the cash. Another customer caught sight of the money, grabbed him outside the pizza place, and took the money. Kimball gave chase and caught the guy, who put up a fight. Being $1,400 rather than $14, it was worth a real struggle, and the thief pulled a knife, sticking Kimball in the right hand and deeply gashing his palm.

The cops arrived and initially thought Kimball was the thief.

"Were you trying to buy drugs?" they asked him as they broke the two up.

"I don't even do drugs. This guy took my money," he told the officer. The money was gone. That night, Kimball played the gig with a large bandage on his hand. The show must go on.

●

Two months before the album came out, Touch and Go released a seven-inch single, "Here We Go Again" backed with "Candy," a standard marketing move to hopefully help album presales and give a taste to radio and magazine people.

Life of Crime came out in September. Touch and Go produced a total of 7,200 units, including 3,100 CDs, the first time the Hyenas had been available on the emerging medium. The vinyl press was roughly 3,000 copies, with 1,882 cassettes.

Compared to the previous Hyenas records, "we went all in," Rusk says. "The songs were so good, we felt it might reach beyond their previous audience."

The same week it was released, the band was interviewed by Cleveland-based *Alternative Press*, a substantial music publication launched in 1985 before the term "alternative" came to represent a major-label genre as it did in 1990. The idea was to chronicle underground music, but it grew into a de facto tip sheet for recruiting labels. Landing an interview for the Hyenas was a coup.

Asked what makes *Life of Crime* fresh, Strickland credibly said it was "another picture of the band captured at this time," adding that it was not as "bluesy as the last one."

Kimball chimed in when the interview asked about the intensity of the live show.

"Everybody's got a lot of aggressiveness and anger about life, so we use that," he said. "It comes easy to us as it's just the way that we feel. There's a lot of craziness in the band, and we kind of live one day at a time because you never know what's going to happen. We're just trying to hold things together and make it through because sometimes things get way out of control."

Monroe added that the current tour was going well, but

that "we might break up tonight or tomorrow, or we might stay together for twenty years. I mean we have goals, but all of those things are insignificant when the band breaks down and someone ends up dead."

Larissa on stage at the Casbah in 1990.
Courtesy of Grace Kennelly.

It was mythmaking, and it didn't seem contrived for readers of a magazine that was putting Nine Inch Nails, Killing Joke, and its colleagues on the cover.

The Hyenas also did a three-page interview with *Maximum Rockandroll*, which had evolved from a sometimes-critical look at music into an advocacy fanzine. Good press was a sure thing.

The interviewer asked Brannon about why the band was started. Rather than deal with the Birthday Party epiphany he had mentioned before to other inquisitors, he said, "We had a deep feeling inside of ourselves that we wanted to kill people, we wanted to commit crimes, we wanted to sell drugs, we wanted to fuck up every God damn motherfucker in the world. At that point, we figured we could do that or start a band. So we started a band."

The interview broke off for a separate discussion with Strickland. Asked what she thought of *Life of Crime*, this time she said, "I'm not sure. It takes a while to decide what I feel about it. I'm really pleased with it, mostly. Personally, I'm not really crazy about the direction. I think our best record is *You Can't Pray a Lie*. That had a more raw edge to it, and we were doing things that were a lot different. Now I think it's more up front, maybe too up front. That's only my personal opinion, not the whole band's."

The reviews for *Life of Crime* again came in positive.

Jersey Beat, which had previously panned the band, noted in its review that Strickland's guitar was masterful: "That one guitarist can do so much is indeed impressive . . . this band totally works together to flail out and reach the heights of its wild rock ugliness."

In the same issue, a reviewer named the Hyenas gig at CBGB as one of her favorites of the year, along with shows by Jane's Addiction, Ministry, and White Zombie, popular company to keep.

The Rocket, a biweekly that ably covered the local music scene in Seattle, praised *Life of Crime* as "scary music . . . but not something you want to turn away from . . ."

"As ever the Hyenas pour out their little dark hearts with such honest hoarseness amid the right rhythms and rumbling bass that you are really glad to know them but not personally," the review said.

A broadsheet put out by KUCI, a college station operated by the University of California, Irvine, noted that *Life of Crime* "truly kicks all the way through . . . and they aren't even from Seattle."

Ben Is Dead out of Los Angeles wrote that it was "bluesy grunge" and "the vocals have the 'too much whiskey tonite' screech of Killdozer, which combines well with the medium tempo slop not unlike other label mates the Jesus Lizard. You know by now if you would like this or not. I do."

The first thing Preston Long noticed about hanging out with Brannon and Strickland was how people would just bring them beer and pot and "whatever."

Long had attended high school in nearby Ypsilanti, enlisted in the US Navy, then got out and wondered what was next. He came to Ann Arbor to attend the University of Michigan, "and that didn't work out," so as he flunked out, he got a job as a cab driver.

"That's where I met Kevin, who I thought was kind of a dandy and an asshole and a smart ass," Long says. "We got along. And the next thing I know, he was crashing on my couch."

Long was the singer in a local band, Wig, an unambitious but surprisingly good combo that had a single out, as did any group that could raise $500.

Long began hanging out with the Hyenas, drinking beer, listening to music.

"John had this amazing video collection, TV stuff from I have no idea where," Long says. "I mean, Stooges, Alice Cooper, Birthday Party, anything you wanted, he had it, and some of it was really rare."

Long was learning the guitar and would play and try to get Brannon to sing along; "since he had this great voice, I would strum the chords to any Rolling Stones song and he could sing it, not 'Brannonize' it, [but] in a really calm, low voice."

Sub Pop Records was at the top of its game in late 1990. The Seattle-based label was cranking out some of the most popular indie music in the world, led by a roster that included Mudhoney, Tad, Nirvana, and the Afghan Whigs.

Its Sub Pop Singles Club was a subscription service that sent members a monthly seven-inch, which often became collectible immediately, usually based on both the rareness and the high quality.

Label cofounder Bruce Pavitt in 1983 began writing a column for *The Rocket*. The column, titled "Sub Pop," was an index of local and national music he felt merited attention.

In February 1988, Pavitt took notice of the Hyenas and *Merry Go Round*, sticking it at the top of a list he called "Kill the Pain / more stuff to check out."

So the Hyenas were on his map, and he'd met them as they came through the Pacific Northwest on tour in 1990. An idea was hatched for a special edition seven-inch package for the Singles Club in which four bands would cover an Alice Cooper song. The Hyenas were the perfect band to join Sonic Youth, These Immortal Souls, and Gumball for the project.

But first, they had to put together a song. Which one?

The band had been working on Cooper's "Public Animal #9" off the 1972 *School's Out* LP. It was ambitious if only for the fact that it had a twisting lead guitar line, which was not how Strickland played. Laughing Hyenas songs had no leads, much like the Ramones or the Fall.

It was suggested that Long handle the part.

"As talented as she could be, she didn't take being held to task to learn shit," Long says. "I couldn't play, but I was willing to sit down and try and I'd eventually be able to play it."

The band worked through it with Long on guitar, not well, but by the time they tried it live, at the end of a September show at CBGB in New York, Monroe, Kimball, and Brannon had it nailed. Long and Strickland missed notes and chords, but it was a passionate rendition.

"I think Larissa was a half step off the whole song, playing an E-flat while we were playing in A," Long says.

They had a couple of weeks to hammer it out at home in Ann Arbor, as they were due to head to Smart Studios again to cut the track.

While they were home, the band played the Heidelberg again and Strickland did an interview with the *Michigan Daily*.

It wasn't a smart or insightful conversation, and she said much the same things she had before. She acknowledged that music is probably not going to be a career for the band.

"If you make it a career, you are prostituting your music," she said. She picked one of four roads the Hyenas could take for the future.

"We can get really popular or end up dead, in jail, or as teachers and scholars," adding, "We're not Rhodes scholars, we're road scholars."

By the time they got to Madison, "Public Animal" still wasn't ready; it took repeated takes until it sounded right. Long was no Glen Buxton and Strickland was no Michael Bruce. But the final cut of the song came out sharp and loud, just as much Hyenas as Alice. While there, they recorded another song, "Don't Bogue My High," a *Pray*-era tune, for a scheduled Touch and Go tenth anniversary sampler.

Setlist from the Life of Crime tour. Courtesy of Kevin Monroe.

From Madison, the Hyenas worked their way South, through Iowa, Kansas, and down to Texas, where they met up with Sonic Youth at Club Clearview in Dallas for the first of five shows together.

The Hyenas blistered the paint on a Thursday night in the Deep Ellum section of Dallas, a scathing show that drew screams and screeches of appreciation from the full house, which was presumably there to see Sonic Youth play songs off their new LP, *Goo*.

"I want all of you to run over an armadillo for me tonight," Brannon told the crowd as the band ended its set.

The next night was Houston, followed by Austin, then a swing west to include a show at the Warfield Theatre in San Francisco before returning to the Midwest and playing a gig at Detroit's Saint Andrews Hall in downtown, Brannon with his hair newly cut and Monroe barefoot and sans beard. The band again raged. No matter the offstage drama, the drug habits, and the discontent, they never seemed to have a bad show.

Openers in Detroit were again Wig, which was becoming a brother band.

They were getting so close that Monroe and Kimball were jamming in their off-hours with Long as a three-piece. They were doing less distorted, country-tinged songs backed by Kimball's insistent beats.

It was just for fun, though. Surely nothing would come of it.

SIDE 7

" Me and Larissa got into a fistfight onstage," Brannon says, recalling one thorny incident during the summer of 1991. "We had a real Sonny and Cher thing going on for a couple of years."

It was, to be kind, a bad breakup.

The Laughing Hyenas were still as alive, intense, and driven as they had ever been. But the decoupling of Brannon and Strickland caused undue tension on the long van rides that the four Hyenas had reconciled as their fate.

Life of Crime was a critics beacon, catnip for Hyena fans, but was dwarfed by a surprisingly fertile talent pool in the indie music ranks.

Nirvana in October 1990 had picked up a new drummer, Dave Grohl from Washington DC's Scream, and was moving to the top of the pack, thanks in part to producer Butch Vig's talents.

Sonic Youth was opening arena shows for Neil Young & Crazy Horse.

Mudhoney was being approached by major labels but opted to record one last record for Sub Pop in the spring of 1991.

Even Touch and Go was seeing some explosive new acts take hold.

In February, the second Jesus Lizard album, *Goat*, was released to rave reviews and the band was headlining packed houses.

"There was an inkling that things were not really happening for the Hyenas when *Goat* came out and Jesus Lizard took off," says Bruce Adams, who was working for Touch and Go. He had a front-row seat to the emergence of the new bands, and no one was moving like Jesus Lizard.

"[Jesus Lizard] went on tour with a huge amount of shirts and records, and very quickly were having to order more," Adams says, indicating merch sales that were far eclipsing what the Hyenas were mustering. "They were doing this like no other Touch and Go band was."

Chicago's Urge Overkill released their final Touch and Go full-length, *The Supersonic Storybook*, in March before signing to Geffen. In the fall, Urge was chosen as the opening band by Nirvana for nine dates on the European leg of the *Nevermind* tour.

The major labels, backed with millions of corporate cash, were signing anything with an amp. Outfits with absolutely no commercial potential—Foetus, Melvins, Babes in Toyland—were getting tens, even hundreds of thousands of dollars thrown at them, only to be dropped or to disband after lackluster sales.

The Smashing Pumpkins and the Lemonheads were likewise courted by majors, all bands that were more palatable and well-behaved.

The Hyenas were neither of those things.

The best the Hyenas could do was an overture via letter from a new label, Interscope, which had formed via a merger of a film production operation and Atlantic Records.

"Right when they were starting out, they approached us," Brannon said years later on *Turned Out a Punk*, a podcast documenting music history hosted by musician Damian Abraham.

"They sent us like this kind of form letter saying, 'We are a new company called Interscope and we're approaching you because we're looking for exciting new bands,'" Brannon said. "At that point, we're still holding on to our, you know, 'We're independent, man; we're Touch and Go.'"

Brannon was aware that the Hyenas had limited commercial potential as well.

"I think a lot of people were turned off by my voice," he said. "It was going on, right at that point was kind of . . . the alternative pop sound. [We] don't sound like the Beach Boys and the Beatles; we're coming from the Stooges and Birthday Party . . . so we were the anti-that and what was going on."

Separately, Brannon says at one point, "Sub Pop was really on our dick. We were hanging out with [Sub Pop cofounder] Bruce Pavitt, totally tripping doing mushrooms, and he's like, 'I gotta get you on my label. No bands on our label have an edge.'"

"At this point we were total derelicts," Brannon says. "We were outlaws number one. For what it's worth, we were the biggest drug addicts. Lived and fucking partied the hardest, played the hardest. But we meant it. It was probably the realest shit out at that whole point."

Kimball and Monroe, though, were decidedly not drug addicts by the end of the *Life of Crime* dates. They moved out of Ann Arbor and into Detroit.

"I felt as if I were getting closer to thirty years old and

we weren't producing enough music," Monroe says. "I felt I could not get Larissa motivated at that point and she was spinning her wheels in a bad way, complaining about her health. Do drugs, don't write songs. I don't care about the drugs, but the songs . . ."

The whole Hyenas thing was getting old for him.

Brannon and Strickland remained in Ann Arbor, battling fierce heroin habits, living separately.

"They were like this couple that had cooled out, but then Larissa would get volatile, make threats," says Jim Magas, the musician who had befriended both the previous summer. Strickland had been staying intermittently with Magas until her drug habit wore him out. It was about money; she didn't have any.

Despite the personal crises, the Hyenas played plenty of shows, but the venues and the money remained pretty much the same.

"They never made that jump to headliners at pretty big clubs," Adams at Touch and Go says. "They could play [Chicago's] Lounge Ax or [Minneapolis's] Seventh Street Entry as headliners, but they wouldn't make a lot of money."

Still, Adams loved the band: "I made no bones about how happy I was to work their records."

While the Hyenas didn't have any new original songs to record in 1991, the Alice Cooper Sub Pop Singles Club release came in June, two seven-inch singles packaged together in a black-and-white wrapper. The Hyenas version of "Public Animal #9" was widely regarded as the best of the outing; it was by far the most ambitious. It was backed with Sonic Youth's cover of "Is It My Body," with bassist Kim Gordon singing. The other single featured Gumball carrying out a rousing "Under My Wheels" and These Immortal Souls doing an adequate "Luney Tune."

"The Sonic/Hyenas disc is splendid and the other is surprisingly unadventurous," reported Seattle free throw *The Rocket*.

The live shows remained profound, masterfully held together by a two-two equation—Kimball and Monroe creating the heaviest rhythms, while Brannon and Strickland went crazy in drug-fueled frenzies.

"That was the horror of touring," Brannon says. "We always tried to, like, leave with enough [heroin], but you're going to run out in Nebraska. I would always try to portion my shit out."

When Strickland ran out, "that's when the fights started. 'I know you got this shit.' I'd be like, 'Fuck!'"

The band reached the East Coast in the summer of 1991 to play Maxwell's in Hoboken, New Jersey, a now-familiar venue to the band.

The occasion was a slot opening for Thee Hypnotics, a British band on UK indie label Beggars Banquet, who was touring in support of the well-performing album *Soul, Glitter & Sin*.

It had been a while since the Hyenas had played Maxwell's, and the house was filled with local musicians.

"I saw Kim from Sonic Youth, Jim Foetus, Cristina from Boss Hog," recalls Magas, who was in New York on a visit and met up with the band to hang out and get a ride back to Michigan.

The band hit stage and erupted, Strickland crouching in front of her amp to coax feedback, swinging her guitar around while Brannon anchored himself five feet from the lip of the stage, twisting his head in time to his delivery.

The band was at the top of its game. Even though the music world was going mad with money and praise for anyone who could potentially move units, the Hyenas were just there for the music.

Kevin Monroe at Maxwells. Photo by Ken Salerno.
Courtesy of John Brannon.

They were so popular in metro New York that the headlining Hypnotics, who hustled the Hyenas to remove their gear from the stage, played to a half-empty club. Everyone had come to see the Hyenas.

"I want to thank you for getting everyone to leave" the singer told Brannon, mistakenly thinking they had chased the crowd away.

"Whatever," Brannon replied, too polite to point out everyone had come to see the Hyenas.

After the show, the band stayed at the apartment of the Dustdevils, a New York band with a strong reputation in the underground music world, with extra cred for being among the first bands released by Matador Records, an East Coast indie label.

Their place was near the corner of Rivington and Ludlow, in Manhattan's Lower East Side, where the cover of the Beastie Boys' *Paul's Boutique* LP was shot.

"We stayed a couple floors up," Brannon says. "We stayed there a few times. The Puerto Ricans were all out there, so dope was easy. We had money and we stayed close."

The next morning, the band was getting ready to head back to Ann Arbor. Magas and Strickland were up early and hit a bodega that had, of all things, fresh apple pie. Strickland's love of apples made her breakfast decision easy. They got their food and went back to the steps outside the apartment, Strickland blissfully stoned.

"She'd take a bite, or try, and I'd watch it, very slowly, move up to her mouth," Magas says. "Then it would fall off her fork. Then her arm would drop. Then she'd do it all again, over and over. She was really a mess."

After a while of this, the band came downstairs with their bags.

"Okay, let's go," Brannon said.

"I'm driving," Strickland said.

"Ahhhhh," Magas said under his breath.

"No, you're not going to drive," Brannon said, likely as high as she was. "Kevin is going to drive."

"No, I am. I'm going to drive," she insisted.

A routine fight ensued.

"It wasn't my place to say," Magas says. "And she was still the mom, the manager of the band. She was high but still managing."

She took the wheel, and they headed toward the Holland Tunnel and the ten-hour drive home. Strickland fell asleep at each stoplight, then awoke in time to move to the next light.

"Finally we stop for gas, and they were all still fighting over who was going to drive and anything else," Magas says.

"I'll drive. I really feel like driving," he announced to everyone. It was agreed, a neutral party to handle the ignition.

After getting on the Interstate 80 turnpike, everyone fell asleep.

Magas: "Then they'd all wake up and start fighting again. That band could really fight."

They came home and did yet another local show at the Heidelberg, a blistering set with New York band Unsane as openers. In September, they hit Bogart's in Cincinnati, a showcase club near the University of Cincinnati. It set off one fawning female admirer, who tried to put her feelings into print via *Rifle Comix*, a magazine presented by WRFL, the University of Kentucky's student-run station.

"John Brannon's awesome contemptuous presence loomed directly overhead, sweating hate, screaming the pain of love. . . . The band finished their set all too soon with terrible fury. Their black boots left the stage: the altar of emotional sacrifice, and I was left crushed, gasping, panicked once again that they might never return. My whole world was the Laughing Hyenas for sixty eternal minutes. I wanted to burn in their hellfire forever."

A month later, the band played Phantasy Nightclub, a Cleveland joint that locals Devo and the Pagans, among others, had played at various points.

"The best band I have ever seen, shit ever WILL see," a reviewer with fanzine *Grumblebutt* reported. "Brutal, consuming, devastating from first drunken note to last bleeding howl. Sincere brutality, not that watered-down street-level shit act that so many of today's artists are trying to dump on us. There was no effort, no fronting act, no tougher-than-nails rhetoric; these are scary people playing what comes naturally. It doesn't matter, they aren't trying to convince you."

They still had it.

Then they got in the van and drove back to Michigan, another quiet drive. They had to get home, as Strickland had to catch a flight to Florida, where her mother was battling cancer and needed help.

Strickland had been going back and forth from Florida during much of the year, putting an occasional crimp in their touring.

Monroe rented a room in a house in the West Village neighborhood of Detroit with several musicians, including Preston Long, the Wig vocalist who had left the band and moved to Detroit.

As Strickland was gone and the Hyenas were on a brief hiatus, Monroe, Kimball, and Long continued to jam. Soon they began to put together some songs as a three-piece at the Hyenas practice space.

"There was a lot of friction with Larissa over the drugs," Kimball says. "[The Hyenas] didn't have any new material. And so when we weren't practicing, we dicked around with Preston."

Once she returned, they always tried to wrap it up before Brannon or Strickland arrived for Hyenas practice, Long says.

On one occasion, Strickland showed up while they were finishing, surprising them.

"I heard you guys were going out with a country girl," she said to them, alluding to the chatter that the trio were working up a batch of songs with a country flavor.

Not only was she right, but Kimball and Monroe, one night and out of the blue, announced they were leaving the Hyenas.

"Kevin and I had done these country-based songs, and we had Jim come in and just play on them," Long says. "And there was still a weird dynamic between John and Larissa, and they had broken up. So Jim kind of came over to us. It was a pretty clean break. They left the Hyenas together."

It was not a confrontation; it was simple declaration: Monroe and Kimball were done with the Hyenas.

Brannon was "not real happy about it," Monroe says. "It was like breaking up with a girlfriend or something. It was like leaving someone you care about, but you can't go on with."

Kimball contends he talked Monroe into leaving. "I was like 'Fuck this, let's try this new band,'" Kimball says. "There was already so much baggage. The drugs were catching up. It was still very painful to leave."

The new band was called Mule.

And with that, the Hyenas were no more. For a few weeks, Brannon and Strickland considered the end, even as Strickland told friends that they weren't done.

"Me and John decided to go on with the Hyenas all the same," Strickland wrote to Al Crim, a longtime friend of the band, on December 23. Her knack for drama often gave her communications a breathless tinge and, on this night, she was particularly theatrical.

"I just can't give up, Al. In three months I'll be 32 years old, and my parents are beginning to think maybe I am mentally ill, still trying to play dumb punk rock music. Am I? Maybe so. Right now I am writing you from the graveyard shift of a Texaco Food Mart, the night before Xmas eve. Light breeze swaying the palm trees, listening to Louis Armstrong on the radio."

She closed her letter with best wishes and "I know you are busy, but please stay in touch."

SIDE 8

It took a week after Strickland returned from Florida to get back on track.

Brannon called Todd Swalla, former drummer in local hardcore heroes the Necros.

Swalla had known Brannon and Strickland for over a decade, having shared bills with Brannon's Negative Approach dozens of times.

He was a no-frills, dexterous drummer, a timekeeper. Rather than inducting a stranger into the transient lifestyle of the Hyenas, Swalla came with road experience, having toured nationally with the Necros. He also had some recording chops, playing on two full-length LPs and a smattering of singles with the band.

He was living in his native Toledo when he got the call. The answer was a quick yes.

For a bassist, Brannon tapped his network.

"You know anybody who plays bass?" Brannon asked several of his contacts. Then he remembered a guy in Cleveland who was a regular at Hyenas shows. He was always effusive, an "I really dig you guys" type of fan who always wanted to talk with the band.

"Who is that guy who hangs out, name is Kevin?" Brannon asked Tom Dark, a local musician in the Cleveland area. "Doesn't he play bass?"

He did. As with Swalla, it took one call.

"Yeah, I'll come to Ann Arbor. I'm not doing shit," Kevin Ries told Brannon.

He came to town before Strickland's return, and he and Brannon worked on some songs. And a bonus: Ries was a drug user.

"I mean, it's not always the best union," Brannon says. "But that's how we were rolling in those days. At that point, I was desperate to put together a band and I know Corey [Rusk, at Touch and Go] was like, 'You guys gonna put out a new record?'"

Brannon, Swalla, and Ries jammed a few times and did some low-key shows as the John Brannon Blues Experiment. Strickland returned from Florida, and the Hyenas were back.

They spent the next few weeks "basically writing new material and getting a set down," Swalla said in a YouTube interview with Brian Walsby, an illustrator and chronicler of the punk scene.

"I was a little intimidated having to play his stuff," Swalla said, referring to Kimball's licks. "We don't play alike at all. I eventually learned those songs on my own terms. And then we had new songs anyway."

Within months, they'd come up with four new songs and a cover of "Solid Gold Hell" by Australian band the Scientists. They'd done some dates, including a West Coast swing, and Ries and Swalla were playing well.

The band made plans to record a new EP before Strickland

was to book a US tour. They would go south and then west, taking in the Midwest, Texas, Arizona, California, and up to Seattle.

Records and T-shirts were on order to sell along the way.

Ries, though, was being evasive. He'd met a woman in Los Angeles during their tour. She'd come back to Ann Arbor with him. And she wasn't going to stay home while he was on the road.

As the tour dates shaped up, he announced a request: He wanted his girlfriend to come along as the merch girl.

Bands usually have strict rules about taking partners on the road, and that rule is "No."

While the Hyenas may have picked up and dropped off people in exchange for drugs or money, a partner in the van was an invasion. The van was the house, the only sanctuary band members had while visiting strange towns and encountering stranger people.

It was a place to sleep, listen to music, get high, and get to the next venue.

Bands would sometimes take roadies, who would serve as all-around assistants, fetching anything from guitar strings to drugs. They would usually double on the merchandise table, selling what they could to add to the coffers.

But those people were not romantic partners.

Taking a girlfriend was a deal-breaker.

"We told Kevin that was not going to happen, but we had these songs," Brannon says, referring to the four tunes that had shaped up and were ready to record.

Would Ries agree to at least stick around to lay down the tracks? He agreed to do that.

Before Ries could change his mind, Brannon told Rusk they were ready to go into a studio to record the new stuff.

But it wouldn't be done at Smart Studios again.

Butch Vig had become a nationally celebrated producer, having worked on the Smashing Pumpkins album *Gish* followed by Nirvana's *Nevermind*, both certified platinum—over a million sold.

As the Hyenas prepared to record the new songs, Vig was finishing up Sonic Youth's next LP, *Dirty*. His schedule was jammed, and his rate was high.

The Hyenas were trading a national profile for a local one; Vig had broad appeal and national acclaim. Brannon had heard of White Room Studios on the third floor of a ten-story building in Detroit's Capitol Park Historic District, in the middle of downtown. Making the record locally would be a good idea, he thought.

Producer Al Sutton was building a reputation as a guy who could deliver the noise. He had recently produced *Face*, by Big Chief, the band original Hyenas drummer Mike Danner had migrated to after leaving the Hyenas.

Rusk booked four days for the band to record at White Room over the July Fourth holiday in 1992, starting on Friday the third. The band was immediately happy with Sutton's approach—hands off, let them play.

Sutton was no novice to the sound, as he'd seen the Hyenas several times and was especially impressed with the *Life of Crime* LP.

The new members, Swalla and Ries, were as dead-on as their predecessors.

"There was no preproduction; they came in and did it, no fucking around," Sutton says. "They laid down those songs in one or two passes."

The band dynamics weren't as durable as the work ethic. Brannon was still hopelessly addicted, and Strickland was trying to kick, slamming coffee, her nerves on edge.

"It was a very dark chapter," Sutton says. "The tension between [Brannon and Strickland] couldn't have been higher. I had never been in a situation where any two people argued more. And it wasn't even about the music, they were just fighting. John was nodding out, Larissa was very frustrated and hyper-focused on playing her parts. She had this intensity that I had not seen in my career to that point. And her intensity wasn't for fun. She was fighting for her life to make this record."

Bassist Ries, the short-timer, replaced former drummer Jim Kimball as the odd man out.

"He was kind of a mystery," Sutton says. "He was a little out of place, clean-cut, not at their level of dirty. There is a darkness to those guys, and I don't mean that disparagingly. Like the darkness of Miles Davis. You don't make that kind of music without something bouncing around in your soul."

The EP, *Crawl*, came out in October.

Somehow, Ries's image was not part of the cover art, which featured a black-and-white illustration, again by cartoonist Bill Widener. For *Crawl*, there were just three Hyenas pictured on the back cover.

Ron Sakowski had been around the Detroit scene for over a decade, most recently spending time as Swalla's bandmate in the last version of the Necros from 1983 to 1988. He was rangy and thin, sporting a shoulder-length tangle of reddish-brown hair and a friendly, easygoing demeanor. Sakowski was also a strong player. He was not nearly as artistically flamboyant and animated as Monroe, but he had a reliable, steady hand.

Like Swalla, Sakowski had extensive road and studio experience, and the idea of putting him and Swalla back together was appealing to Brannon and Strickland.

"Todd called me one day and asked if I was interested, and before I could even agree, John called me the next day," Sakowski says.

"I'm sending you a tape so you can learn the songs," Brannon told him. Sakowski was essentially drafted as a Hyena.

"I was a fan of the band; I knew the songs in my head," he says.

Ron Sakowski at Stache's, Columbus, Ohio, November, 1992.
Photo by @jfotoman. Courtesy of John Brannon.

He had two weeks to learn and rehearse the songs before a show at the Blind Pig in Ann Arbor, then the band took to the road to promote *Crawl*.

Over the rest of 1992 and through 1993, the band hit the same spots it had been hammering for the past half decade:

Sudsy Malones in Cincinnati, Khyber Pass in Philly, the Lounge Ax in Chicago, whatever new place was opening in New York. They went to the West Coast and back, scraping together low-end gigs with the occasional higher-profile opening slot.

The shows were still strong; Swalla and Sakowski managed to rock the older songs, and the newer material was slower and well crafted.

But Brannon and Strickland remained dogged by their habits, and they were wearing out. Swalla, too, picked up a habit, he acknowledged to the *Detroit Metro Times*.

The Hyenas were coming to terms with the fact that their career, mission, pursuit—whatever it had become—wasn't moving forward.

"At that point, we had toured so much [that] nobody lived anywhere," Brannon says. "We had really just given up everything. We'd go to 7-Eleven, and we would be in some of the magazines, but we couldn't afford a Slurpee. Larissa would be on the cover of *Alternative Press*, and we couldn't afford to buy the magazine. We were street people."

They rolled into Los Angeles for a series of shows in late 1992, crashing on couches around the city. A couple of generous hosts were also cat owners, so Strickland had to find somewhere else to stay because of her feline allergy.

She decided to get a room at the River Glen Motel, best known as the place Quentin Tarantino used for Bruce Willis to hide in *Pulp Fiction*.

"God, this place is creepy," Strickland said when the band picked her up the next morning.

Brannon was shooting dope in the back of his hand and carried his clothes in a garbage bag. Strickland was dope sick or high constantly, a ying-yang of ornery and pleasant.

"We would hook up with all these crazy chicks and people, gave them rides to the next town," Brannon says. "We were like, 'What the fuck?' We were bored and we never had roadies, so we figured, 'You got some gas money? You got some weed?' Yeah, you can roll with us. They'd always freak out hanging out with us. We were kind of shady."

John and Larissa on stage at Stache's in Columbus, Ohio, November 1992. Photo by @jfotoman. Courtesy of John Brannon.

The year 1993 blurred into 1994 and shows in lofts and basements became as common as their regular small-venue stops.

At the same time, their guarantees began to decrease. The bands that were signed to major labels and previously accepted $500 guarantees could now demand more money.

If you wanted to book Alice in Chains, there was a chance you'd also have to book a lesser-known band from the same promoter for a little more money. It was an unspoken practice in the industry known as block booking, which had been quashed off and on through litigation dating back to the early twentieth century. It was still a thing.

The corporations that ran labels like Sony, Capitol, Warner Bros., and Atlantic funded tours that, if they failed, could be tax losses. But big business would only endure so many losses. Bands signed to majors a year earlier were being dropped.

A&R people jumped up in every town, it seemed, to replace those castoffs with the next big thing.

"It gave me the impression that labels put out a bounty to bring bands," says Michael Gerald, bassist/vocalist with Killdozer.

Other than the query from Interscope sent two years before, no one was interested in the Hyenas.

The shows began to slide. Tempos would vary, and Strickland was showing signs of wear and tear. She was puffy and moved slower. Worse, the Hyenas were now incorporating traditional blues songs into their set, drawn-out time wasters including a dull-as-dirt version of John Lee Hooker's "It Serves Me Right to Suffer," complete with a guest harmonica player—Strickland's new boyfriend, Terry, who was doubling as the band's road manager. The "no partners" rule had clearly gone out the window. They threw in another grinder, "I Want You Right Now," a tune first played by the Troggs in 1966 as "I Want You" and covered better by the MC5. In the hands of the Hyenas, it was a dull filler song that went on endlessly.

In the parlance of the recovery community, the Laughing Hyenas had hit bottom. The shows drew the faithful but the band had no chance of turning the corner. No bigger venues and no larger guarantees were in the cards.

Buried in the muddle of looming failure, a refreshed version of the band, against all odds, took hold.

Brannon was writing songs, emboldened by material he was taking from his deterioration, both personal and physical.

In March 1994, at a show in Muncie, Indiana, the band played several new songs. "Just Can't Win," "You're So Cruel," and "Each Dawn I Die" were featured, sounding astoundingly fresh. Brannon wasn't doing the usual 100 mph scream but instead tempered his delivery. The band let down on the older songs, but when these new songs came along in the set, they pepped up.

Larissa Strickland, John Brannon, Ron Sakowski, Todd Swalla.
Touch & Go promo shot. Photo by Ewolf.

By June, the Hyenas were getting close to having the material for a full-length, adding several more songs mostly written by Brannon. Their work ethic remained taut, and their constant roadwork had helped hone the songs.

One of the songs was called "Hard Time Blues," and the new record became *Hard Times*. Where to record was a question, but they had options.

Working with Al Sutton had produced a sonically strong EP, but Brannon and Strickland had heard *Extra Width*, by the Jon Spencer Blues Explosion, the band Spencer formed after the demise of Pussy Galore.

The sounds were experimental and bluesy. The new Hyenas material was slowed down and likewise bluesy. *Extra Width* was recorded partly at Easley McCain Recording in Memphis.

"We were at this point where we were like, 'Damn, man, we gotta get into the studio," Brannon says. "We couldn't afford Butch Vig, but we're still on Touch and Go. Spencer told me, 'Dude, I did this record at this studio in Memphis,' and that's what I wanted to do."

Strickland worked out the deal with Rusk and booked the studio in Memphis.

"Larissa wanted to put something out and said, 'We're recording at this place in two months," Sakowski says. "She made us cooperate and hammer out these songs. We were practicing two or three times a week, getting things tighter."

In mid-June 1994, the Hyenas rolled into Memphis, ready to record *Hard Times*.

Easley McCain had been up and running since 1990, decked out with a twenty-four-track board.

"We were inexpensive, and so bands could come to town and not have to pay out the wazoo," says co-owner Davis McCain, who had previously run sound at the Antenna Club, a regular stop for national bands and a popular place for the local bands to land support roles and some exposure.

It was a large room, and the Hyenas spent the first day loading in their gear, including the PA stack Brannon sang through on every record.

McCain noticed Brannon was talkative and nervous, voicing reservations about how it would go.

"Obviously, there had been this period where they had not recorded for a while and he was nervous about whether it was going to be what it was or if it was gonna suck," McCain says. "He wasn't sure they were going to pull it off."

The band showed no signs of drug use, he says, something he would notice after spending years of working at the Antennae Club.

He was right; Brannon, Strickland, and Swalla were kicking, Sakowski says.

"I planned ahead and brought a bag of weed to record. Even Larissa took a puff. But they hadn't had heroin for a while."

Strickland was quiet as were Swalla and Sakowski. "Businesslike," is how McCain puts it.

"They came in pretty prepared; they had their songs pretty much in line and knew what they were going to do," McCain says. "John had the songs ready to go."

Brannon says the band could nail the songs that were already written, but "we kind of told Touch and Go that we had the [full] album written, which we didn't. I wrote a couple of those jams in the hotel room. You could probably tell if you listened to that record. For "Slump" Larissa had the riff, but we did that in the hotel room the day before we recorded. I had no lyrics. We didn't even have the change; I think I wrote that. We wrote that shit in literally half an hour."

They also cobbled things together in the lounge at the studio, in the van in the parking lot, or anywhere they could string parts of songs together. The Johnny Cash cover, a stinging version of "Home of the Blues," for example, was born in the van; they'd never done the song before recording it.

"It was the song we pulled out of our brains," Sakowski says.

Their version is propelled by Sakowski's acoustic guitar with an assist from studio co-owner Doug Easley on pedal steel.

The album was wrapped in five days at a cost of $3,242.

It marked a dramatic change in the band's sound. The new rhythm section carried the day, led by Swalla and Sakowski, who together performed with a precision and heart that was only eclipsed by the maturity of Brannon's voice, no longer just a scream but a varied instrument.

"Larissa would also comment to John, 'Don't scream, stop screaming, you've got a nice voice,'" Sakowski says. "And after a while, he put on his singing voice."

The album's cover art for the first time featured a photo of the band, taken in Detroit by local photographer Eric Wheeler, who went by Ewolf—a shy, quiet artist who had shot numerous covers for numerous indie labels, along with major magazine spreads.

He was a pro.

When the band showed up for the shoot a couple of months after the recording was made, "they described what they wanted," he says. "They wanted an older, almost, not quite Blue Note but like a classic Rolling Stones photo."

No one in the band was into the *Hard Times* photo session, Brannon says.

"We showed up and were all fighting," he says. "Larissa was saying she wouldn't do it if Todd was there, and I had just kicked dope, and I was feeling crappy. They told us to all wear suits, so of course none of us did."

Ewolf had to run home and retrieve his own suits, drums, guitar, and microphone.

"So Ron is wearing my shirt, tie, and jacket; Todd is modeling with my snare drum, this old Slingerland sixties snare drum; Larissa is playing this old Harmony hollow body that I had; and John's holding this old Shure microphone."

The resulting cover was an arresting shot of a band that looked elegantly spent.

Touch and Go optimistically produced nearly 2,000 vinyls; 5,500 CDs; and 1,100 cassettes.

And Brannon could barely function. He was on the heels of a breakup with his girlfriend of four years, Julie Jumonville, also an addict.

Julie Jumonville and John Brannon. Courtesy of Julie Jumonville

The end was a drug story.

In late 1993, as Brannon was beginning to write some of the songs that would appear on *Hard Times*, Jumonville realized her addiction was going to end badly. She wanted to get straight.

"I didn't have insurance, and so there was no rehab that way for me," Jumonville says. "My mom found me a place in South Carolina that would take me for free, so I left with this fantasy of getting clean, then John was going to get clean and we're going to live happily ever after.

"I waited for a year for him to get clean and he didn't."

The breakup was devastating for both.

"I was just at the end of my rope in every way," Brannon says.

SIDE 9

"John Brannon doesn't scream anymore!" a *Hard Times* review opened in German-language magazine *No Trend Press*. "The irrepressible anger of the early records has given way to a bluesy melancholy. . . . *Hard Times* is a new Laughing Hyena experience that you will either hate or love."

"Very bluesy disc recorded in Memphis for added effect," came the verdict from *Under the Volcano*, a Long Island publication. "Singer John Brannon moans these songs like a man who has truly suffered."

The Boston *Phoenix*, on the other hand, was fooled into thinking the Hyenas had gone straight: "Given that the Laughing Hyenas have stuck together for a decade through adversities that would have decimated the resolve of lesser indie-rock proles, they can be forgiven the release of a merely okay album. . . . [I]t is befuddling that the four-years-in-coming *Hard Times* . . . finds them scrubbed clean and with a solid line-up . . . [and is] a departure from past triumphs."

And finally, an obscure Czech magazine asked a poignant question: "Laughing Stones? Rolling Hyenas? Serious Trouble?"

Even a gem has its critics.

In late February 1995, the Laughing Hyenas gathered at Zoot's Coffeehouse in Detroit's Cass Corridor for one of several shows that month in preparation for a tour starting in April to promote *Hard Times*, which came out in late January.

The band onstage at Zoot's Coffee House. Courtesy of John Brannon.

The tour was to include fifty shows in two months across the US. But the band was in bad shape.

"We laid down the album," Brannon says. "And I put myself in rehab. I just knew we were gonna do a big tour and I was having a breakdown. I was like, 'I can't live like this anymore.'"

Strickland, though, "she never stopped."

Before the Zoot's show, longtime friend of the band Tim Caldwell had been commissioned to do an interview for *Seconds Magazine*, an East Coast newsstand mag with some heft.

Zoot's was a converted Victorian home turned coffee

shop featuring stained overstuffed chairs and a chipped wooden floor where the bands played ingloriously at eye level with the crowd.

The Hyenas had just put out a monster of an album and toured with some of the giants of the industry, but they had not moved forward. On their home turf, they were just another band. They were agitated, wondering what it would take.

Strickland started the interview off with a diatribe against "the press," angered over the idea that anyone would call *Hard Times* a blues album.

"I think a lot of people are like, 'So why'd you guys decide to do a blues album in Memphis?'" she said. "Well, I mean, it's like we'd been feeling it already, you know what I'm saying? And it was really, like, just maybe three songs, I think, have a traditional blues change in [them], a progression."

It was a pedantic rant that set the table for a lowbrow conversation from a band that was fielding praise and criticism for what was one of its best releases. Caldwell deftly handled the petty complaints.

It was the first time, though, that they claimed the reason for the departure of bassist Monroe and drummer Kimball was because, according to Strickland, "John and I had written *Crawl*, and Kevin and Jim didn't want to play *Crawl*."

The lineup change meant little, Strickland added.

"I think that it's the same band, as far as musical direction and roots."

The band was taking everything very seriously, including themselves. After ten years together, Brannon and Strickland had battled dope, a corporate takeover of post-punk, and each other. The years had hardened their view of almost everything, and outside the windows of the van things appeared to conspire against them.

The current lineup had been in place for almost three years, and *Hard Times*, which should have opened some eyes, was just another platter in a product onslaught, sitting next to the latest Pearl Jam escapade or Stone Temple Pilots fiasco.

As the interview closed after nearly an hour, Strickland called attention to something few would have known about without her mentioning it.

"I want to dispel all the recent publications really quickly here and say that I am alive, and no, I did not die two months ago from a drug overdose, as was printed in *Thorazine* and a local fanzine called *Jam Rag* and I guess also in a couple Australian obituaries," she said. "I'm fine, thank you very much."

Caldwell never turned in the interview for publication.

A couple of weeks later, the *Michigan Daily*, which had faithfully documented the Hyenas as deserving hometown heroes, ran an interview with Brannon and Strickland along with its *Hard Times* review.

"We're trying to put everything that's happened behind us and hopefully gain a better attitude towards things," Brannon told the interviewer. "We just want to get out there and play with nothing standing between us. We do fifty shows in two months. I'm sure it will kill us, but we've done it before. Larissa's not dead and we're all ready to go."

It didn't go well.

"The *Hard Times* tour was impossible," Brannon says.

"We played the shows, but everyone was fighting. Ron was still pissed at Todd for taking his $900 bass and pawning it for dope money. Todd said he wanted to write a song and so Ron was cool, he handed over his bass to give him something to write on. Four months later, he asks for it back and Todd just says, 'I don't have it.'"

The shows varied. Some showed flashes of the old Hyenas reckless abandon, while others were going-through-the-motions exhibitions.

A couple of weeks into the journey, at a stop in Fort Worth, Texas, "Just Can't Win," one of the standout, energized tracks on *Hard Times*, became a flaccid low-tempo dirge, the band standing rooted to the stage, Strickland staring at her guitar, Sakowski looking like he'd rather be anywhere else. Brannon and Swalla gave their best, but the team was not functioning.

"Of the tours I have been on, it was not the most spectacular," Sakowski says. For one thing, it was grueling: almost every night in a different town for a batch of people in their late thirties, several of whom enjoyed their intoxicants with vigor.

"Getting everyone on the same page for some of the shows was hard," he says. "In any town where they knew they could score, bang, that was the first thing those three did. Sometimes when they were strung out, I was playing bass and everyone else was getting ready to nod off."

They got back to Detroit and Swalla bailed.

"I quit," Swalla told *Detroit Metro Times* in 2018. "I wanted to get away from drugs, basically. So I had to get away for a time if I wanted to get my act together."

It was common for bands to not speak for weeks after a tour. They'd been pent up in a van for months with each other. But in this case, weeks turned to months.

"No one ever said, 'Let's stop this,'" says Sakowski, who went back to his wife, his job hanging drywall, and paying the bills.

"It just kind of stopped," he says.

Strickland moved back to Florida to care for her ailing parents. Brannon nursed his habit, picked up after an unsuccessful rehab stay. He could barely function.

The last years of the band, despite the underrated *Hard Times* album, took the heart out of Strickland.

John Brannon with his mom and Louis the cat.
Courtesy of Julie Jumonville.

"She was just kind of doing it for me," Brannon says. "The last couple years she's like, 'John, I'm done.' Well, we were, you know. But I'm never going to give up. I said to her, 'Well, nothing else is going on in our lives.'"

The Laughing Hyenas had everything going for them when they began: looks, attitude, chops, personality.

It wasn't the drugs alone that sunk them. It was the timing. The industry had changed into a profits-first enterprise, and bands that thrived catered their sound to the changing culture and corporate demands.

Bands that held the fort, the Hyenas among them, remained artistically intact but were destined to play small rooms for small money.

The Hyenas, though, would have had a hard time with Nirvana-style fame.

"I don't think they could have handled it," says Al Sutton, who produced *Crawl*. "They walked through those doors on occasions and were freaked out by it. You had Sonic Youth touting them. That wasn't blowing smoke. Some just can't make that step."

Butch Vig has seen fame screw up some artists. But whether the Hyenas could have handled it, "we'll never know. But they had a hard time just navigating life at the level of success that they had."

There was no sentimental burial for the Hyenas. Brannon struggled with heroin for several more years, at one point spending time in jail. Yet he managed to stop using even as various rehab programs had failed him—"I had to do it myself," he says. Brannon formed Easy Action shortly after the Hyenas' break, and in 2006 he also began touring with a version of Negative Approach featuring Sakowski on bass.

Strickland wandered in and out of the music scene, never playing but bouncing around between Florida and the Midwest. She remained hopelessly addicted, although there were clean moments. In 1998, she married a Ukrainian man in Port Charlotte, Florida, where they lived in the house her parents had left her.

Strickland was found dead at home on October 9, 2006, a Monday. The cause was reported to be an "apparent" overdose of the prescription drug Xanax. She'd lived a life of mostly self-induced hardship, primarily due to the illness of addiction.

In 2018, Third Man Records, a label and enterprise founded by Detroit music impresario Jack White, rereleased the Laughing Hyenas catalog. Done in cooperation with Touch and Go Records, the move was a favor to the ears of everyone.

There were no illusions of riches, as so many other older bands who have gotten the reissue treatment dream of.

Some wrongheaded notions of a bastardized version of the Hyenas playing fresh dates were quashed quickly by Brannon.

"Without Larissa," he says, "it's not the Laughing Hyenas."

CODA

The Laughing Hyenas were a cult band. John Brannon, a formidable and recognizable front man as well as a Detroit music icon, has realistically acknowledged that for decades.

His stature as a hardcore singer, blues moper, and seasoned screamer has earned him some deserved respect.

Yet, even after the Hyenas achieved their epoch, Brannon had to battle for appreciation. He had earned it, for sure. It took some time to get the word out.

The story goes—and it sounds apocryphal but hang in—Brannon was at Off the Record, a record store in the Detroit suburb of Royal Oak, in the late nineties, flipping through CDs like any other music fan. A teenage punk-rock kid in his late teens stepped up to flip next to him.

When Brannon saw the kid pull a Negative Approach CD from the bin and examine it, Brannon said, "Hey, man, check it out, that's my old band." Noticing Brannon's long greasy hair and strung-out look, the kid peered at him sideways and said, "Fuck off, hippie."

It's a cool anecdote, an occurrence that almost anyone who has reached cult-icon status has endured.

For them, anonymity is always one trip to the local Kroger away.

Thankfully, Brannon can shrug it off. He's indie rock royalty, the good guy made good, a rare and pleasing accomplishment. Anyone who encounters him comes away with a good feeling, and that means something today.

Some of the material used in these pages came from interviews, some previously run, for another book I wrote, *Detroit Rock City: The Uncensored History of Rock 'n' Roll in America's Loudest City* (Da Capo, 2013). The people I spoke with for that book were mostly honest and forthcoming, a respectable trait that is increasingly rare.

I met some good people on this ride, some in person and some via the sad but necessary email, text, and phone. Bruce Adams, a talented wordsmith who was a roadie for the Hyenas, has a terrific memory. Jim Kimball, who drummed for the Hyenas in their heyday, is a real character, which makes conversation enjoyable and challenging. Mike Danner, the first Hyenas drummer, is a solid soul who relished being part of a larger story.

Thanks to Jim Magas, who remains an underrated talent, and is always worth spending time with. Check out his music wherever finer taste is available.

Kevin Monroe is a life-of-the-mind fellow and someone you would want in your foxhole.

John Brannon is a gentle soul who deserves every accolade that comes his way. He has realized his art his way, without pandering or reaching for the dime. If only we had more artists like that.

Corey Rusk is among the many who deserve more than

just thanks. Without his integrity and purity of vision, Touch and Go Records would never have achieved its deserved status as an iconic symbol of the nineties music scene. He has never wavered from a simple notion: It's the music, stupid. He stuck with the Hyenas despite their bad habits, gave them plenty of room to be themselves, and the records speak for themselves, each one a true piece of art.

Special thanks to Tim Caldwell, whose emails are their own world. He was knowledgeable and helpful in this endeavor.

And many more thanks to Al Crim, Ben Blackwell, Dave Buick, Peter Davis, Michael Gerald, Julie Jumonville, Rick Lieder, Preston Long, Davis McCain, Rick McGinnis, Knox Mitchell, Chris Moore, Tony Rettman, Ron Sakowski, Rob St. Mary, Al Sutton, Todd Swalla, Third Man Records, Butch Vig, Andy Wendler, and Eric Wheeler.

Special nod to Chris Fuller. He's always scanning.

There is more to be written on the Laughing Hyenas, and big props to anyone who undertakes or has undertaken the noble task. Doug Coombe's oral history of the Hyenas published in the *Detroit Metro Times* in 2018 is an excellent place to start. Anything written on the band deserves to be read by anyone who wants to remember when rock 'n' roll was unfiltered and didn't need the blessing of The Man.

NOTES

SIDE 1

Doug Coombe, "L-Seven Is the Detroit Post-Punk Band That Time Forgot—but Third Man Records Is Looking to Change That with a Deluxe Reissue," *Detroit Metro Times*, August 19, 2020, https://www.metrotimes.com/music/l-seven-is-the-detroit-post-punk-band-that-time-forgot-but-third-man-records-is-looking-to-change-that-with-a-deluxe-reissue-25157958.

Ian Johnston, *Bad Seed: The Biography of Nick Cave* (Little, Brown, 1995).

SIDE 2

"Award-Winning Community High School Jazz Musicians," *Ann Arbor News*, May 12, 1984, https://aadl.org/taxonomy/term/168024.

"Laughing Hyenas Live on WCBN Radio," Ann Arbor, Michigan (June 22, 1987), https://www.youtube.com/watch?v=L6lfpZHBb2U.

Matt Calrson, "Laughing Hyenas Struggle Against the Hard Time Blues," *Michigan Daily*, March 9, 1995.

SIDE 3
Bruce Adams, *Your Flesh* magazine, no. 15 (1989).

SIDE 6
"If you make it a career, you are prostituting your music": Kim Yaged, "Laughing Hyenas Share Their Gift," *Michigan Daily*, October 10, 1990, https://digital.bentley.umich.edu/midaily/mdp.39015071754860/434.

SIDE 7
"Right when they were starting out, they approached us": Damian Abraham, *Turned Out a Punk* (podcast) episode 362, https://www.youtube.com/watch?v=m5KfFcWj44k&t=365s.

SIDE 8
They spent the next few weeks "basically writing new material and getting a set down": Brian Walsby, "Self Empunishment Chat with Todd Swalla," https://www.youtube.com/watch?v=JRz-twwGDVc.

Doug Coombe, "An Oral History of the Laughing Hyenas, One of the Great Unsung Detroit Rock Bands," *Detroit Metro Times*, December 12, 2018, https://www.metrotimes.com/music/an-oral-history-of-the-laughing-hyenas-one-of-the-great-unsung-detroit-rock-bands-18664679.